Frontend Architecture for Design Systems

A Modern Blueprint for Scalable and Sustainable Websites

Micah Godbolt

Beijing · Boston · Farnham · Sebastopol · Tokyo

Frontend Architecture

by Micah Godbolt

Published by O'Reilly Media, Inc., 1005 Gravenstein Highway North, Sebastopol, CA 95472.

O'Reilly books may be purchased for educational, business, or sales promotional use. Online editions are also available for most titles (*http://safaribooksonline.com*). For more information, contact our corporate/institutional sales department: 800-998-9938 or *corporate@oreilly.com*.

Editor: Meg Foley	**Indexer:** Judy McConville
Production Editor: Nicole Shelby	**Interior Designer:** David Futato
Copyeditor: Jasmine Kwityn	**Cover Designer:** Randy Comer
Proofreader: Rachel Monaghan	**Illustrator:** Rebecca Demarest

February 2016:   First Edition

Revision History for the First Edition
2016-01-25:   First Release

See *http://oreilly.com/catalog/errata.csp?isbn=9781491926789* for release details.

978-1-491-92678-9

[LSI]

Table of Contents

Part I. Origins

Part II. The Code Pillar

Part III.   The Process Pillar

Part IV. The Testing Pillar

Part V. The Documentation Pillar

Preface

Conventions Used in This Book

The following typographical conventions are used in this book:

Italic
> Indicates new terms, URLs, email addresses, filenames, and file extensions.

`Constant width`
> Used for program listings, as well as within paragraphs to refer to program elements such as variable or function names, databases, data types, environment variables, statements, and keywords.

`Constant width bold`
> Shows commands or other text that should be typed literally by the user.

`Constant width italic`
> Shows text that should be replaced with user-supplied values or by values determined by context.

 This element signifies a tip or suggestion.

This element signifies a general note.

 This element indicates a warning or caution.

Who This Book Is For

This book is not a technical manual, though there are plenty of code samples along the way. This book is not purely theoretical, though it spends as much time dealing with *why* we do things as it does on *how* we do things. Therefore, the audience for this book is neither the developer who is simply looking for technical answers, nor the project manager who only wants the 5,000-foot view.

The audience for this book is the developer who wants to better understand the bigger picture of frontend development. I'm writing this to energize and inspire developers to take up the mantle of the frontend architect and fight to make the frontend a first-class citizen in their next project.

It is also written for technically minded managers who are trying to wrap their heads around the ever-changing landscape of frontend development. This book will present compelling arguments for the inclusion of various tools, standards, and best practices that can elevate a project's frontend development to a whole new level.

Using Code Examples

Supplemental material (code examples, exercises, etc.) is available for download at *https://github.com/micahgodbolt/front-end-architecture*.

This book is here to help you get your job done. In general, if example code is offered with this book, you may use it in your programs and documentation. You do not need to contact us for permission unless you're reproducing a significant portion of the code. For example, writing a program that uses several chunks of code from this book does not require permission. Selling or distributing a CD-ROM of examples from O'Reilly books does require permission. Answering a question by citing this book and quoting example code does not require permission. Incorporating a significant amount of example code from this book into your product's documentation does require permission.

We appreciate, but do not require, attribution. An attribution usually includes the title, author, publisher, and ISBN. For example: *"Frontend Architecture for Design Systems* by Micah Godbolt (O'Reilly). Copyright 2016 Micah Godbolt, 978-1-491-92678-9."

If you feel your use of code examples falls outside fair use or the permission given above, feel free to contact us at *permissions@oreilly.com*.

Safari® Books Online

 *Safari Books Online* is an on-demand digital library that delivers expert content in both book and video form from the world's leading authors in technology and business.

Technology professionals, software developers, web designers, and business and creative professionals use Safari Books Online as their primary resource for research, problem solving, learning, and certification training.

Safari Books Online offers a range of plans and pricing for enterprise, government, education, and individuals.

Members have access to thousands of books, training videos, and prepublication manuscripts in one fully searchable database from publishers like O'Reilly Media, Prentice Hall Professional, Addison-Wesley Professional, Microsoft Press, Sams, Que, Peachpit Press, Focal Press, Cisco Press, John Wiley & Sons, Syngress, Morgan Kaufmann, IBM Redbooks, Packt, Adobe Press, FT Press, Apress, Manning, New Riders, McGraw-Hill, Jones & Bartlett, Course Technology, and hundreds more. For more information about Safari Books Online, please visit us online.

How to Contact Us

Please address comments and questions concerning this book to the publisher:

O'Reilly Media, Inc.
1005 Gravenstein Highway North
Sebastopol, CA 95472
800-998-9938 (in the United States or Canada)
707-829-0515 (international or local)
707-829-0104 (fax)

We have a web page for this book, where we list errata, examples, and any additional information. You can access this page at *http://bit.ly/front-end-architecture*.

To comment or ask technical questions about this book, send email to *bookquestions@oreilly.com*.

For more information about our books, courses, conferences, and news, see our website at *http://www.oreilly.com*.

Find us on Facebook: *http://facebook.com/oreilly*

Follow us on Twitter: *http://twitter.com/oreillymedia*

Watch us on YouTube: *http://www.youtube.com/oreillymedia*

PART I

Origins

In the beginning was the Web, and the Web was good. Well, in this case, the beginning was the early 90s, and "good" meant a site had found its way onto the Yahoo! index page and the visitor counter was spinning at the bottom of the table-laden, animated GIF–infected page.

But that's all you really needed in those days. As long as you were feeding your fellow webring subscribers with click-throughs, all of the webmasters were happy. And those webmasters? Yes, they were masters of their domain...literally! Websites were simple creatures, and the webmaster was their keeper, tending to the tangle of HTML and wondering if these new Cascading Style Sheets were something to be bothered with; most had already written off JavaScript as a passing fad.

But like any medium, the Web grew. JavaScript stuck around. CSS was useful for more than just setting the page's font family and font color. Webmasters eventually found themselves at a crossroads. Their website traffic continued to grow, and the technologies of the Web continued to expand (transparent GIFs!). There were too many new things to keep track of, too much work to do; eventually webmasters were forced to specialize. On one hand, they really liked their "under construction" signs, and the ubiquitous marquee tags, but on the other hand Perl was the best language ever to be created and will undoubtedly power every website from here into eternity.

When it came to hiring a second person to help run their precious domains, webmasters needed to decide if they wanted to continue to be <blink> tag masters and hire Perl script kiddies, or the other way around.

Eventually these decisions had all been made, and the modern web team began to assemble like a news team called to a large seashell. At every stage, every crossroad, former webmasters found themselves needing to focus on a smaller chunk of the web process. Some of them focused on serving files over a server, while others improved their skills in accessing a database, while still others found joy in creating graphics and images.

Newer, more focused roles also attracted artists, writers, business analysts, engineers, and mathematicians to the industry. As these roles developed, and their members become more and more proficient, the Web began to form a new set of designations...or disciplines.

Those Who Strategize About Content

Early on in the development of the Web, there was a particular personality that believed the words on any given page were as important as the design, the code, or even the search engine optimization (everyone knew that keyword stuffing was the way to go). Before they came along, content had always been a problem to deal with later. "Just throw some lorem ipsum into the design and move on." The client will eventually fill it in with real, quality, inspired content before the site goes live...really...always.

These lovers of words were ultimately quite vocal that the Web was content, and that this content deserved our time and attention. It was always a battle, but they began to be invited into early planning meetings, and on occasion asked to develop editorial strategy. They were making progress! The fight was difficult and lonely, but the results were worthwhile.

Thus went each of these lone warriors until the fateful day where they happened to come across another logophile, and they realized that they weren't alone in this struggle! This kindling of a friendship quickly grew into a blaze of new connections. Eventually a community was formed, and they continued to focus their efforts on convincing others to treat content as a valuable asset.

Years passed and the fight for content was far from over. But even as one more designer was asked to "just make something up" for the homepage copy, a new rallying cry could be heard in the distance. December 16, 2008, was the day that Kristina Halvorson stood up high atop the "A List Apart" blog (*http://alistapart.com/article/thedis ciplineofcontentstrategy*) and raised a banner for content strategy. She asked us all to "take up the torch" and begin "treating content as a critical asset worthy of strategic planning and meaningful investment." Those who practice content strategy were to "Learn it. Practice it. Promote it." They were to become content strategists. And like that, a discipline was born.

Kristina's article was not the first one to broach the topic of content strategy, but it was the first to define the heart, soul, and purpose of content strategy. Overnight, this group of word disciples had been given a name for their collective calling. These disciples would usher in an era of blogs, podcasts, and conferences revolving around the simple notion that "content mattered."

A Responsive Web Was Born

Around the same time, a man in a black turtleneck got up on stage and utterly ruined everyone's conception of what an Internet-connected device was. For the first time in the history of the Web, we were forced to accept that websites were not browsed solely on 1024 × 768 pixel screens in the comfort of our offices and living rooms with the fat pipes of broadband Internet. The introduction of the iPhone ushered in a new era of web-connected devices with a multitude of screen resolutions, varying capabilities, fluctuating connection speeds, and inconsistent input modes. As developers, we could no longer make assumptions about our user and the properties of the device they were using to view our websites.

In response, we tried a number of solutions. We tried relying on pinch and zoom, or double tap to zoom, leaving our sites mostly untouched, or we redirected any mobile device to a stripped-down, mobile-friendly "m.dot" website. Neither solution really solved the problem. Pinch and zoom sites were difficult to navigate in order to finalize purchases or sign up for services, and increasing mobile traffic meant increasing lost revenue. Although m.dot sites were more user friendly for mobile devices, they required development teams to maintain two separate websites.

Many m.dot sites languished, failing to be updated as frequently as their larger siblings, or the reduced feature set of the m.dot site forced users to switch to desktop devices to do anything more than get directions or place a phone call. Something needed to be done. Though some considered the iPhone a passing fad, it was soon quite obvious that the future of the Web lived inside of these small, personal screens.

On May 25, 2010, three years after the release of the iPhone, Ethan Marcotte penned a lengthy article (*http://alistapart.com/article/ responsive-web-design*) on A List Apart called simply, "Responsive Web Design." This article did not describe some new discipline, or a banner for embattled developers to gather under. Instead, it described a method for creating a new breed of website that would respond to the size of the user's device and mold itself to that viewport. Responsive web design (RWD) was not some new or emerging technology, but rather a collection of existing tools and techniques, including the following:

Fluid grids
Percentage-based widths rather than fixed-pixel dimensions.

Flexible images
100%-width images fill the container they are put inside of, and flex as the viewport changes size.

Media queries
Being able to specify different styles for different viewport sizes, we could now change page layout based on the size of the screen.

All of these techniques had been available in the browser for years before Ethan's article, but just like Kristina's call to arms for content strategy, his description of RWD clearly defined the solution everyone was desperately looking for.

In a single article, the web development industry had been transformed.

The Seeds of Frontend Architecture

It was with this history in mind that I started to think about the notion of frontend architecture. As a Drupal frontend developer, I knew full well the frustration that content strategists had felt. The frontend styling was always an afterthought. It was a layer of "pretty" applied to the default markup after the designers and back-end developers had finished their work. The challenges we faced couldn't have been better exemplified than in the order in which people were brought onto a project. I saw projects start, designs debated over, functionality developed...and *then* a frontend developer was pulled onto the project to apply whatever design was tossed over the wall to whatever markup our CMS chose to output.

Having gone through this process several times, I knew the pain I was going to experience as I tried to deconstruct a set of mobile and desktop Photoshop files. The goal was to form them into a theme that could be applied to the div soup that Drupal spit out. Speaking to Rails friends about the challenges of styling a website navigation, I eagerly confessed, "One does not simply change Drupal navigation markup," and it was true! Once that markup was set, and the developer had moved on to another task, the chance of modifying the combination of divs, lists, and links was all but a dream. This inevitably led to some ridiculous CSS hacks to make a design that was never meant to fit the default navigation markup actually work in production.

For many years, frontend developers' worth was measured by their ability to create these Frankenstein-style design patterns. "Now if I put a pseudo element on the third nested div, and use a background image from this sprite..." was our battle plan, and it was terrible. We were patching up holes in a failing levy, hoping that we could launch the site before we got swept away by waves of technical debt.

This process wouldn't be sustainable as the complexity of our projects grew. So instead of doing things the way we've always done them (because they've always worked in the past), I began to imagine how a project would differ if we made frontend development "a critical asset worthy of strategic planning and meaningful investment." What if we had a voice in things like CSS frameworks, documentation tools, build processes naming conventions, or even the markup itself?! I started to wonder what a large-scale project would look like if UX development fed backend development, instead of the other way around.

Would this create a revolution? Would others pick up the same torch and start to "Learn it. Practice it. Promote it."? Before we could all rally under a single banner, we needed to understand what that banner stood for. What should we demand? How could we accomplish our goals? What might we be called?

What's in A Name?

In backend development, where planning and scalability are key, software architects are highly valued. They are invited onto a project long before development begins, and they have discussions with clients about the architectural needs for their soon-to-be-built platforms. What technology stack are they going to use? What are their content types? How is content created, stored, and displayed back to the screen? The role of a software architect is to make sure that nothing is ever created by chance, but rather guided by an overarching architecture.

I realized that what frontend development was missing was architecture. We were being asked to do all our work piecemeal, as an afterthought. It didn't take long for me to convert databases and web servers to Sass folder structures and build systems, and the title of frontend architect was born.

Now, every job title needs a job description. What would a frontend architect do? How would they impact a project given the proper opportunity? These ponderings led to a lightning talk about frontend architecture at my company's annual retreat, and a speaking opportunity at CSS Dev Conf that led me to focus my thoughts into a concise 45-minute presentation.

On October 13, 2014, given to a packed room inside a New Orleans conference center, "Raising a Banner for Frontend Architecture" was a rallying cry for the developers who had already been on the front lines of this fight. I wanted them to know that they were not alone, and that there were others out there to support them and back them up. I spoke to project managers, salespeople, and developers alike, outlining the power of a properly architected frontend and the value that it brought to the team and to the client.

After the talk, I heard story after story of developers who finally understood who they were, and the role they played in their organization. Many people found themselves performing the role of frontend architect, but had never taken on that title, or felt confident enough to ask for the authority the position should carry. The weeks after CSS Dev Conf saw many people changing their Twitter bios to read "frontend architect." And I, being one of those to make the change, haven't looked back since. No matter the title I currently hold at my present job, I am a frontend architect.

CHAPTER 1

The Discipline of Frontend Architecture

Frontend architecture is a collection of tools and processes that aims to improve the quality of frontend code while creating a more efficient and sustainable workflow.

When I think about the role of a frontend architect, I always think about the characteristics that it shares with that of a traditional architect.

An *architect* is defined as someone who designs, plans, and oversees the construction of buildings. This is exactly what a frontend architect does, except that the end product is a website. And just as an architect spends more time drafting up schematics than pouring concrete, the frontend architect is more concerned with building tools and processes than writing production code.

Let's dive into this definition and explore what our role would be as frontend architects.

Design

Think about a building with no clear architecture. The important decisions were all left up to the builders doing the work. One wall built was with stone, another with brick, a third with wood, and the fourth omitted because it was trendy.

The overall look and feel of the website is still squarely in the hands of skilled designers, but the frontend architect crafts the frontend approach and design system philosophy. By designing a system all frontend developers are going to work within, the architect sets a clear vision of what the end product, the code, will look like.

Once a frontend architect sets the vision, the project has a standard against which to test code. Without a design for the finished product, how could we determine whether or not our code actually has met that standard? A carefully designed system will have checks and balances ensuring that all code contributed to that system adds perceivable value, rather than just adding lines of bloat.

Planning

With a clear design in mind, the planning stage involves mapping out the development workflow. What steps will a developer take to write a line of code and see that code through to production? In the simplest case, this plan involves FTPing into a server, editing a file, and hitting Save. For most projects, it will involve some combination of version control, task runners, CSS processors, documentation tools, test suites, and server automation.

The goal of the frontend architect is to design a well-oiled machine that provides quick and painless setup; offers useful feedback in the form of linting, tests, and documentation; and reduces much of the human error that occurs when we perform repetitive tasks.

Oversight

Frontend architecture is never a "set it and forget it" proposition. No design or plan is ever perfect or complete. Clients' needs (as well as the needs of developers) will change and evolve over time, and a process that was working well in one phase of the project might need to be revisited later to improve efficiency or reduce errors.

A key talent of a frontend architect is the ability to continually make those adjustments. Modern build tools make it very easy to change workflows and distribute those changes out to each team member.

Some people have asked if becoming a frontend architect means a role in management, and never writing a line of code again. I can personally attest that not only do I write more code as an architect, but I get to write in a greater variety of languages, and for a larger number of tools. It's not that I write less code, but simply that the audience of my code has changed. A frontend developer's audience is the end user, whereas a frontend architect's audience is the developers themselves.

Adopting an Architectural Process

Just like other disciplines before it, frontend architecture has had to fight a battle of priorities. While we can't imagine why anyone would start building a skyscraper without first consulting an architect, that is in fact how most large web projects start.

The excuses are numerous: We don't have the budget. We don't have the time. We'll make those decisions after all of the designs are done. Or worse, there is no excuse; you are just placed on the project months after the design was finalized and development is already in full swing. You now have just a few months to make a pile of HTML magically look like a stack of PSDs tossed over the wall to you. This is not the way to successfully develop a scalable and sustainable website.

As frontend architects, we believe that there are a number of key frontend decisions that need to be made at the beginning of a project. These decisions are either too difficult to implement later on in development, or the cost of making the wrong decision is way too great. Once those decisions are made, our task is to help shape the visual design, platform development, and infrastructure setup to best meet the needs of our envisioned architecture.

Without the early input of a frontend architect, projects run the risk of having to choose between reworking designs, platform, or infrastructure and telling the frontend developers to make do. I can tell you from experience, betting on the former is always a bad gamble.

What's the Catch?

I know this isn't going to be an easy task. The changes I am suggesting have a tangible cost, and anyone in a position to make these decisions will always need to weigh the risks and the possible benefits. For anyone who hasn't had the experience of working with a frontend architect, this can be a difficult risk to take.

The chicken-or-egg dilemma is that to overcome the objections of spending time and money on a proper frontend architecture, many stakeholders will require examples of how this approach has helped projects succeed in the past. This obviously requires you to have worked on a project like this in the past. How do you get the opportunity to work on a project like this, if you are always required to prove that the approach works?

Fortunately for me, and this book, I was recently entrusted with the task of creating a new design system for a large-scale website. I was given the time to thoughtfully plan out this new system, creating new coding standards, tools, and workflows. Once the project started to take shape, I knew I had a golden opportunity to demonstrate how scalable and sustainable a properly architected design system could be.

CHAPTER 2

Alpha Project

This past year, I was given an opportunity of a lifetime when asked to architect a solution for Red Hat that would let the company share its existing website "bands" across multiple company web properties. Having been on the initial build of Redhat.com, I knew the challenge ahead of me, but I'd also had time to establish the development team's trust, and was given full control over the entire architecture of this project.

I call this an opportunity of a lifetime because it was! Our chicken-or-egg dilemma had been cracked. My team was given the opportunity to build a design system of significant scale, with sufficient technical support, that would eventually be displayed on a site with an incredible amount of traffic. This would be the project that I'd use to promote frontend architecture to my next project...and the project after that.

A Slow, Powerful Start

Our team was incredibly fortunate to be working with Red Hat at that particular time. Having just launched the original site redesign, we were in a bit of a feature moratorium. While we occasionally had a couple of bugs to squash, we were otherwise freed up for months to explore ideas of how we'd architect this new design system.

Despite the sheer amount of legacy code still in production at Redhat.com, we were given a blank slate to work with. Because the website was built on the concept of bands (row after row of unique content), the new elements we built could sit under or over existing bands. There were no sidebar styles to override, no HTML tag styles constantly changing around us. We were practically building a brand-new website right inside the old one. And just like replacing every board on a ship, one by one, we are hopeful that we can eventually retire the old theme system and rely solely on our own.

With such freedom in front of us, we knew we had an opportunity to create a large wish list...and actually get most of it! That wish list included:

Modular content
> We were big fans of Atomic Design (*http://patternlab.io/about.html*), a methodology created by Brad Frost, and wanted to reuse small components rather than creating dozens, or even hundreds, of unique bands.

Comprehensive testing
> We'd been burned too many times by large chunks of frontend code being merged into master, breaking code written months prior. So we were determined to test our design system with the same level of coverage that the application level had.

Streamlined processes
> We wanted to mirror the Git flow system that worked so well at the application level, but we needed to break feature branches into smaller, component-sized code chunks. We also wanted to automate error-prone manual processes we had been doing in the past, like updating style guides, creating icon fonts, and deploying new code.

Exhaustive documentation
> With a large team of frontend developers, backend developers, designers, marketing managers, ops, and various product owners, we had a *huge* audience. We wanted to make sure that whatever we built had documentation that met each one of their needs.

These four areas of focus took us a bit of time to develop, set up, and perfect. There is no denying that our first few months were less productive than they might have appeared if we'd continued building things like we had in the past. But once we got the foundation in place and started building out our system, we quickly realized the power of what we'd built.

With every new request to build a couple of bands, or even a full 12-band page, we found that we had less and less work to do. Instead of approaching each new band as a unique snowflake, we were able to break it down into its smallest parts and determine if any new layouts or components were necessary for our system to build it.

Every story ended with exhaustive documentation, a suite of regression tests, and code that conformed to the standard set down by our original architectural decisions.

Although these tools and processes took some upfront effort, we were literally laughing at how trivial our work had become. Of course, the trivialization of our work was a good thing, as it allowed us to spend less time on repetitive tasks, and pour more time back into our design system. In the end, working inside of this design system was a joy, and with every user story we were excited about how much more powerful it could become.

Armed and Dangerous

Armed with this experience, I am confident that the software we wrote, the processes we created, the techniques we honed, and the lessons we learned will be a sufficient example of success to convince future projects of the validity of this approach.

Using the processes, techniques, and lessons discussed in this book, I hope you can walk into your next project with the confidence to fight for your frontend architecture. Fight to get onto the project earlier, so that you can help influence important decisions. Fight for quality tools and processes so that you can build smarter, more reusable code. Fight to make your frontend design system matter. Take up the banner for frontend architecture, and join the fight with me.

CHAPTER 3

The Pillars of Frontend Architecture

Every building needs a solid foundation, four walls, and a roof. These are nonnegotiable. The foundation holds the walls, the walls hold the roof, and the roof keeps you safe and dry. Any architect who failed to provide these essentials would certainly be considered a failure. As frontend architects, we are under a similar obligation any time we are involved in the creation of a new web property. We are tasked with being champions for the essential tools and processes required to make this website a success.

Working with the Four Pillars

Throughout the rest of this book, we will discuss what I call the four pillars of frontend architecture. These four groups of topics, technologies, and practices are the foundation of a scalable and sustainable design system. They set up a series of discussions that need to be had about the frontend of any new project. These conversations will help to set expectations in code quality, the time and effort needed to finish each user story, and the workflow process that will get all of this done in a timely manner.

These pillars in no way prescribe the only way to do something, or even the best way to do something. Each decision needs to be made in the context of the project that you are in. Sometimes the decision will be to not do anything! Projects of smaller scale, or those that are transient in nature, might not require the same level of foundation as a Fortune 500, customer-facing property meant to last several years.

Do not take the upcoming chapters as a list of topics to master. To be a frontend architect is to be in a state of constant learning. This constant state of learning is what defines us. Our inch-deep, mile-wide understanding of the entire frontend development space is what allows us to be champions for new technologies and methodologies.

One of our strongest skills is that we can spend an hour with a new framework or Gulp plug-in, and identify its strengths and weaknesses and possible use in our project. So if you find yourself overwhelmed by the sheer number of technologies and topics in the rest of this book, just remember that none of us are masters of all of these. I personally range from expert in several of them, competent at many of them, and completely new to others.

So, enough dancing around these pillars, let's dive into them and discuss the significance of each.

The Pillars

The code pillar
> When it comes down to it, every website can be broken down into a bunch of text files and media assets. When we start to look at the sheer number of lines of code produced in the making of a website, it is incredibly important that we set expectations for the code that is written and the assets we create.
>
> In this pillar, we will focus on how to approach the HTML, CSS, and JavaScript of a design system.

The process pillar
> As we are miles away from a workflow of FTPing into a server, editing a file, and hitting Save, it is important to start thinking about tools and processes that will create an efficient and error-proof workflow. Our build processes continue to grow in complexity, as do the tools that we use to create them. These tools bring incredible gains in productivity, efficiency, and consistency, as well as the risk of over-engineering and unnecessary abstraction.

Just as our workflows have evolved, so has the way we work. We are no longer spending our time making the CMS markup "look like" some Photoshop comp. As we move to designing in the browser, and creating responsive HTML prototypes, we are often writing all of the HTML and the CSS before the feature is even implemented in the CMS. This incredible role reversal needs to be supported by a change in development process.

The testing pillar

In order to create a scalable and sustainable design system, we need to ensure that any code we wrote yesterday isn't devalued by the code we write today. Our code isn't written in a vacuum, but rather is part of a much larger system. Creating a plan for sufficient test coverage will ensure that yesterday's code continues to provide the value it did on the day we wrote it.

In this pillar, we will take a look at three different methods for testing our sites. Sometimes, depending on the team size, these tests will be split between frontend, backend, and ops, but a solid understanding of each of them will be valuable when you're communicating with those other teams.

The documentation pillar

It seems that few see the value of spending time on documentation until a key member of the team is about to leave, and then it's "stop everything and document all the things." As a frontend architect, you will be a champion for documentation that is written at the same time as the process or artifact being developed.

This pillar will look at those various types of documentation your team might need to write, the tools used to make publication easier, and the types of end users that will ingest the content.

PART II

The Code Pillar

Good code never happens by accident. It's not that developers are inherently lazy, or that we cannot be trusted, but left to our own devices, we are capable of producing a wide variety of solutions to the same problem. Unlike a trip through a maze, crafting a code solution for a given problem rarely has a single best solution. Each of us tackles a problem differently because we have different experience, opinions, and tendencies.

There is nothing wrong with inconsistencies from developer to developer. It is often our ability to each look at a problem differently that makes our teams stronger. But when it comes to writing those solutions and actually committing something into our design system, there is no desire, or need, for our code to reflect all of those differences.

Even if we could get every developer solving problems in the same way, there is no guarantee that it is the best possible code for the rest of the system. They might be creating a beautiful, well-crafted Bootstrap theme when the project actually called for something much more custom.

The code pillar is here to help us have conversations about the code quality of our HTML, CSS, and JavaScript. It is here to help us define how we are going to write our classes, build our functions, and mark up our interfaces.

The following chapters are nowhere near exhaustive. As a frontend architect, it is your job to continually be exploring and evaluating new techniques, platforms, methodologies, and frameworks. There is no one-size-fits-all solution, but discovering the needs of a new project and matching them up with the current frontend development landscape is what you have been called in to do.

CHAPTER 4

HTML

One of the first challenges you'll face as a frontend architect will be to tackle the markup you want your developers to be writing and your CMS to be producing. The Web doesn't exist without HTML. Strip away your CSS and JavaScript and you will be left with raw content and controls.

Text, images, links, forms, and submit buttons: this is all the Web really needs, and it is the foundation of anything you'll ever create on the Web. Start off with bad markup, and you'll be writing bad CSS and bad JavaScript to make up for it. Start with great markup, and you'll be able to write more scalable and maintainable CSS and JavaScript.

Markup of the Web's Past

It wasn't that many years ago that our approach to HTML markup was something quite similar to laying out a page in a brochure, magazine, or newspaper. It isn't much of a surprise, though, as many of us came from a print background, or were working with designers or product owners with a print background. Before responsive design became the standard (and even some time after), most web properties were treated like a multipage print project. When the work was divvied up, you'd be assigned a page and you would start at the top and work your way down the DOM.

In the past, our markup typically fell into one of two camps: procedural or static. Let's take a look.

Procedural Markup: 100% Automation, 0% Control

In the world of web publishing, it was pretty common for the frontend team to have little to no control over the markup. This was often due to feature development (which included HTML output) being done weeks or even months before the frontend team came onto the project. It was made worse by the fact that the origins of the markup were obfuscated by complex rendering processes, and did not come from a single template. This meant updating the markup was extremely difficult for anyone not familiar with the complexities of the CMS backend. And by that time, the backend developers had moved on to other tasks, and they rarely had time to go back and make any major changes to it.

The effect of this constraint is that CMSes and the backend developers would err on the side of too much markup and too many classes in order to give the "themer" proper hooks into the HTML. In the end, we'd get this:

```
<div id="header" class="clearfix">
  <div id="header-screen" class="clearfix">
    <div id="header-inner" class="container-12 clearfix">
      <div id="nav-header" role="navigation">
        <div class="region region-navigation">
          <div class="block block-system block-menu">
            <div class="block-inner">
              <div class="content">
                <ul class="menu">
                  <li class="first leaf">
                    <a href="/start">Get Started</a>
```

This little snippet, pulled directly from the Drupal.org homepage, shows how your header can have 10 levels of nesting before getting to a single piece of content. The sad thing is that this is a relatively tame example! I can tell you from experience that it can go much deeper.

This "div soup" might have helped us when our job was to match a static Photoshop comp to a page full of markup, but as our needs matured, we longed for more control.

Static Markup: 0% Automation, 100% Control

If we were working on a small project, or simply had a page where we had a huge body field to fill out, controlling the markup was pretty easy. While this situation offered great flexibility, it also meant that we were responsible for maintaining all of the code. Changes that would be simple in a CMS template had to be propagated throughout the pages by hand. So we'd write markup like this:

```
<header>
  <section>
    <nav>
      <div>
        <ul>
          <li>
            <a href="/products">Products</a>
            <ul>
              <li>
                <a href="/socks">Socks</a>
```

To keep things simple, "semantic" markup was preferred, relying on HTML5 elements and their relative positioning in order to apply styles instead of classes. Without classes on our markup, and having been burned by primary navigation styles bleeding down to secondary navigation anchors, we often ended up with long descendant selector chains like this:

```
header > section > nav > div > ul > li > a {
  color: white;
}
header > section > nav > div > ul > li > ul > li > a {
  color: blue;
}
```

This specificity nightmare ensured that every selector we wrote for our hover and active states was at least this long. You don't even want to see how tertiary navigation is styled. Let's move past our past and look at more current practices.

Striking a Balance Between Control and Automation

As the frontend architect, you'll need to evaluate the processes that produce your markup. How much control will you have over the order of the content, the elements used, and the CSS classes applied to them? How difficult will it be to change these things in the future? Are templates easily accessible, or will you need to task a backend developer with the change? Is your markup even based on a templating system? Can you propagate changes throughout your entire system, or is it a manual process? The answers to these questions might dramatically change the way you approach building your HTML and writing your CSS.

Modular Markup: 100% Automation, 100% Control

Theutopian state that we are all striving for is a situation where every line of HTML on our site is programmatically created, yet we as frontend developers have full control over the templates and processes used to create that markup. Unfortunatly, you won't often reach this state. Even in the best situations, there is user-generated content that will have little to no automated markup. Regardless of a CMS's ability to expose HTML templates, sometimes it's just easier to let the CMS determine the markup for things like your forms or navigation. But even if you stand at 90%, a modular approach to your markup will provide you the flexibility you want with the automation you need.

Modular markup differs from procedural markup in that we no longer cede power over to the CMS to determine what markup should be used to output any given content. This allows us to use the same markup for two different navigation instances, even though the CMS might have used completely different markup. Modular markup also differs from static markup in that, being programmatically rendered, it allows us to apply a system of classes to the markup and not rely on the element tags and position to determine their visual appearance. Let's look at that navigation example again with a BEM-style modular approach:

```
<nav class="nav">
  <ul class="nav__container">
    <li class="nav__item">
      <a href="/products" class="nav__link">
        <ul class="nav__container--secondary">
          <li class="nav__item--secondary">
            <a href="/socks" class="nav__link--secondary">
```

At first glance, this approach seems quite verbose! And while I will not argue that point, I will argue that it is the perfect level of verbosity. With a class on every element, we no longer have to rely on styling tags or using element position to determine visual appearance. Compared to the dynamic markup, this markup is much cleaner, and dare I say more "modular"? This navigation pattern could be used in several places throughout the site, using the exact same markup. Therefore, it isn't markup that was created by the CMS and then styled, it is markup that was created, styled, and then integrated into the website's navigation system.

It All Leads to a Design System

So how do we get started with this modular approach? Well, it all starts with changing the way that we create our pages. You see, there is no page. It's a myth. A website page is a relic of our past. What is a page? Is it the content at a certain URL? Well, what is the guarantee that the content at a given URL remains the same each time you visit? What happens if you are logged in? What happens if the content on that page is filtered by the time of day, your location, or your browsing activity? The sooner we realize that we are no longer building pages, but design systems, the sooner we can start to create some amazing things on the Web.

A design system is the programmatic representation of a website's visual language. The visual language, created by our designers, is an artifact that expresses how the website visually communicates its message to users. It is a collection of colors, fonts, buttons, image styles, typographical rhythms, and UI patterns used to convey mood, meaning, and intent.

Just as a spoken language can be broken down into nouns, verbs, and adjectives, our job as frontend developers is to deconstruct the visual language into its smallest pieces. By doing this, we can create rules about how to put it back together again. It is by breaking down the visual language that we learn how to create our proverbial sentences, paragraphs, chapters, and novels. The goal of this conversion is to create a scalable and maintainable codebase that faithfully reproduces anything that the language is able to express.

We'll dive further into creating design systems in future chapters, but it is important that we understand what we are creating, because before we do that, we need to decide how the design system is going to be attached to our markup.

The Many Faces of Modular CSS Methodologies

There are almost as many CSS methodologies today as there are CSS or JavaScript frameworks. But unlike CSS or JavaScript frameworks, which are usually all or nothing and come with a bit of baggage, a

CSS methodology is more of a philosophy about the relationship between HTML and CSS than a prebuilt codebase.

It seems that almost every day you hear about a new approach using some new namespace, leveraging data attributes, or even moving all of the CSS into JavaScript. The great thing about all of these methodologies is that they all bring something interesting to the table, and help you to learn something new about how HTML and CSS can be intertwined.

There is no single perfect approach, and you might find that one project fits best with one, and another project works better with another. There is absolutely nothing wrong with just creating your own methodology, or starting with a popular one and then modifying it to your taste. So if you are wondering where to start when deciding on your own approach, it is best to take a look at a few of the more prominent methodologies, and see what does, and what does not, resonate with the project you are about to tackle.

OOCSS Approach

The following snippet shows the Object-Oriented CSS approach to creating an HTML toggle.

```
<div class="toggle simple">
  <div class="toggle-control open">
    <h1 class="toggle-title">Title 1</h1>
  </div>
  <div class="toggle-details open"> ... </div>
  ...
</div>
```

The two main principles of OOCSS (*http://oocss.org/*) are to separate structure and skin, and to separate container and content.

Separating structure from skin means to define visual features in a way that they can be reused. The simple `toggle` element shown in the preceding snippet is small and reusable in many different situations. It can be displayed using various skins that will alter its physical appearance. The current skin of "simple" might have square corners, but the "complex" skin might have rounded corners and a drop shadow.

Separating container from content means to stop using location as a style qualifier. Instead of styling tags inside of some container, create reusable classes like `toggle-title` that will apply the required text treatment regardless of what element it is used on. This way you can let an H1 look like the default H1 if no class is applied to it.

This approach is very useful when you want to provide your developers with a large set of components that they can mix and match to create their UIs. A great example of this approach is Bootstrap, a system full of small objects adorned with various skins. The goal of Bootstrap is to create a complete system that is capable of creating any UI that a developer might need to put together.

SMACSS Approach

The same toggle component written in Scalable and Modular Architecture for CSS would look like this:

```
<div class="toggle toggle-simple">
  <div class="toggle-control is-active">
    <h2 class="toggle-title">Title 1</h2>
  </div>

  <div class="toggle-details is-active">
    . . .
  </div>
  . . .
</dl>
```

Although it shares many similarities to OOCSS, SMACSS (*https://smacss.com/*) is an approach differentiated by the way it breaks the system of styles into five specific categories:

Base
How markup would look without classes applied to it

Layout
Dividing the pages up into regions

Module
The modular, reusable parts of your design

State
Describes the way that modules or layouts look under given states or contexts

Theme
An optional layer of visual appearance that lets you swap out different themes

In the preceding example, we see a combination of module styles (toggle, toggle-title, toggle-details), submodule (toggle-simple), and state (is-active). There are many similarities between OOCSS and SMACSS in how they create small modular pieces of functionality. They both scope all of their styles to a root-level class, and then apply modifications via a skin (OOCSS) or submodule (SMACSS). The most significant differences between the two (other than the difference in how code is structured in an SMACSS approach) is the use of skins instead of submodules, and the is prefixing the state classes.

BEM Approach

Finally, here is the same toggle component written in Block Element Modifier syntax.

```
<div class="toggle toggle--simple">
  <div class="toggle__control toggle__control--active">
    <h2 class="toggle__title">Title 1</h2>
  </div>

  <div class="toggle__details toggle__details--active">
    ...
  </div>
  ...
</dl>
```

BEM is the third methodology we are going to look at, and is on the other side of the spectrum from SMACSS. BEM is simply a class naming convention. Instead of dictating the structure of your CSS, it only suggests that every element is labeled with a class that describes the following:

Block
    The name of the parent component

Element
    The name of the element inside of the block

Modifier
    Any modifier associated with the block or element

BEM uses a very terse convention for creating these class strings, which can become quite long. Elements are added after a double underscore (e.g., toggle__details) and modifiers are added after a double dash (toggle__details--active). This makes it very clear that `details` is an element and that `active` is a modifier. The use of a double dash also means that your block name could be `news-feed` without confusing `feed` for a modifier.

The advantage of this approach over OOCSS or SMACSS is that every class fully describes what it accomplishes. There are no `open` or `is-active` classes. While those classes make sense in their context (in a `toggle` element), outside of that context we don't have a clue what `open` or `is-active` means. While a BEM approach might seem redundant or overly verbose, when we see a class of `toggle__details--active`, we know exactly what it means: the `details` element, inside of the `toggle` block, is active.

Choosing What Is Right for You

In the end, the only thing that matters is to find a solution that works for you. Don't choose a convention because it's popular, or because another team is using it. All three approaches give you extremely similar tools to work with, and will integrate with a design system in very similar ways.

As I will discuss in Chapter 7, at Red Hat we settled on a mix of SMACSS and BEM. So don't be afraid to experiment, combine ideas, or come up with something completely unique! Just be aware of the prior art, be able to express why your approach will solve the challenges your project faces, and have a team willing to commit to a single, unified approach. If you decide to use OOSMABEM, then more power to you! I look forward to reading about it.

CHAPTER 5

CSS

One of the greatest things about this industry is that we can freely sit down with fellow developers and have a cup of coffee. That might not seem like a big deal, but let me tell you, it is! We work in an industry based on open standards, open source software, open information, and open learning. The tools and techniques we use may be changing at an incredibly fast pace, but working in such an open industry is the key reason we're able to keep up with them. Now this may surprise you, but there are other industries where you would never, ever sit down with a fellow practitioner to talk shop, unless they were paying you to do it. In these industries, every piece of knowledge, every trick, every preset, every macro, every document, and every shortcut is up for sale, and the last thing you'd want to do is sit down with a potential competitor and freely trade that information.

Now compare this to the Web. We thrive on sharing knowledge. We publish blogs, record video tutorials, create public code repos, write on Stack Overflow, respond to questions on IRC, and distribute CodePens, Gists, Sassmeisters, JSbins, and Pastebins, all so that others can learn the things that we know. Getting a cup of coffee and discussing your views on current web practices and new CSS frameworks is the most basic expression of how we share knowledge and how we learn in this industry.

So yeah! We work in an industry where inviting an associate out for a cup of coffee is not only acceptable, but also a valuable practice! These cups of coffee can lead to learning new things, new business connections, new jobs, and even great friends. Suffice it to say, many years of talking shop over cups of coffee, beer, tea, or kombucha has led me to believe that the simple social interface of sharing a beverage is one of the greatest assets we have in this industry.

The great thing about having consistent caffeine- or alcohol-fueled conversations with other developers is that we always have a pulse on what people are excited about, and in what direction they are headed. This is important to me not because I depend on others to know what to do next, but rather because I am able to validate the things I am learning and the discoveries I myself am making. Every year I look back at how my approach to CSS has evolved. So whether my newest obsession is preprocessors, build tools, style guide–driven design, or component-based design systems, I'm always excited to find that others are coming to the exact same discoveries.

The CSS I am writing today looks nothing like what I was writing even three years ago. After each site build, I learn something new and try to apply that to my next project. It's a very organic process of gathering the things I've learned with the things I've read, and trying to apply an improved approach to the unique problems I face. Each iteration brings a marked improvement in my technique, and my understanding of a scalable and maintainable design system.

Along with each iteration are the excited conversations with various coworkers, industry colleagues, or random conference goers. With each of those conversations, I'm consistently amazed that I was not the only person to have a euphoric epiphany about using data-attributes, or opt-in styles to handle my component variations.

As a frontend architect, you might not need to know every tiny CSS bug in some obscure version of Opera mini, but you do need to understand the major trends in CSS, and be able to put together a plan that will set your team up for success. If you haven't been keeping up on the current CSS trends, or your euphoric epiphanies aren't coming as fast as you wish they would, try grabbing a few more cups of coffee with fellow developers, or spend a bit more time doing the "social track" at your next conference. But before you do that, read the following sections so you can get caught up on where we were in CSS a few years ago, why it didn't work, and where we are now.

Specificity Wars and the Pains of Inheritance

It wasn't that many years ago when we were still dealing with the 100% dynamic or 100% static markup that I described in the previous chapter. Regardless of the side of the spectrum we were on, the effect on our CSS was that we almost always started from a global scope and worked our way down, getting more specific with each new level of the cascade. We'd start with general styles on each element, like our header and paragraph tags, and then apply specific styles to the elements inside of the various sections of our page:

```html
<body>
  <div class="main">
    <h2>I'm a Header</h2>
  </div>
  <div id="sidebar">
    <h2>I'm a Sidebar Header</h2>
  </div>
</body>

<style>
h2 {
  font-size: 24px;
  color: red;
}

#sidebar h2 {
  font-size: 20px;
  background: red;
  color: white;
}
</style>
```

Now every H2 is red, except for the sidebar where the H2 is white with a red background.

This concept was easy to understand and made a ton of sense if you were coming from a print background. Every time you put an H2 in the sidebar, it would be styled the same—well, that is until we came across a calendar widget in the sidebar that should be using the original header colors and no background. But that's OK! We could just add another class and overwrite the offending sidebar styles, right?

```html
<body>
  <div id="main">
    <h2>I'm a Header</h2>
  </div>
  <div id="sidebar">
```

```
      <h2>I'm a Sidebar Header</h2>
      <div class="calendar">
        <h2>I'm a Calendar Header</h2>
      </div>
    </div>
  </body>

<style>
h2 {
  font-size: 24px;
  color: red;
}

#sidebar h2 {
  font-size: 20px;
  background: red;
  color: white;
}

#sidebar .calendar h2 {
  background: none;
  color: red;
}
</style>
```

The issues with this approach are numerous:

Specificity
Whether you're dealing with ID tags or just long selectors, over-writing a selector always requires some attention to the level of specificity.

Resetting colors
To get back to the original H2 color we have to specify it again, as well as overwrite the background.

Location dependence
Now our calendar styles are dependent on being in the sidebar. Move the calendar to the footer and the header size will change.

Multiple inheritance
This single H2 is now getting styles from three different sources. This means we can't change the body or sidebar H2s without affecting the calendar.

Further nesting
The calendar widget might have other H2s inside of individual calendar entries. Those H2s will need an even more specific selector, and will now be dependent on four sources for its styles.

A Modern, Modular Approach

Our discussion of HTML in Chapter 4 foreshadowed a few of the modern, modular tenets that the majority of frameworks are employing to deal with the problems we saw in the approach just described. While OOCSS, SMACSS, and BEM have differing opinions about the exact markup to use, each offers advice about how to write your CSS that will be valuable regardless of the approach you take. Let's take a quick look at a few of those key tenets and how they help solve the problems we had before.

OOCSS brings the idea of separating container from content, where we learn to stop using location as a style qualifier. There is nothing wrong with having a sidebar on your site, and to style that sidebar in whatever way you'd like, but the influence of those sidebar styles stops once you get down to the contents of the sidebar. `#sidebar h2` means that every H2 element placed in the sidebar is going to have to either accept or fight off the styles applied by that selector. `.my-sidebar-widget-heading` means that a single heading in the sidebar can opt in to that style, while other modules in the sidebar have headings that are left completely untouched.

SMACSS brings us the idea of separating our layout and our components into completely different folders, further dividing the role of the sidebar and the role of the calendar module. Now that we have defined the sidebar's role to that of just layout, we don't even allow element styles inside of that Sass partial. If you are going to place something in the sidebar and want to have it styled, that element needs to be part of a component, and defined in the component folder.

BEM, while not necessarily a CSS methodology, teaches us the value of having a single source of truth for every class used in our markup. Instead of classes that ebb and flow depending on their context or proximity to other selectors, each BEM class can be traced back to a single set of CSS properties unique to that selector:

```
<body>
  <div class="main">
    <h2 class="content__title">"I'm a Header"</h2>
  </div>
  <div class="sidebar">
    <h2 class="content__title--reversed>
"I'm a Sidebar Header"
    </h2>
```

```
  <div class="calendar">
    <h2 class="calendar__title>"I'm a Calendar Header"</h2>
  </div>
</div>
</body>

<style>

/* Components folder */
.content__title {
  font-size: 24px;
  color: red;
}

.content__title--reversed {
  font-size: 20px;
  background: red;
  color: white;
}

.calendar__title {
  font-size: 20px;
  color: red;
}

/* Layout folder */
.main {
  float: left;
  ...
}
.sidebar {
  float: right;
  ...
}
</style>
```

The issues we had with our original location-based styles are fixed:

Specificity
Changing your IDs to classes is a good start in stopping the specificity wars, and flattening every selector's specificity to "1" allows us to stop using the specificity "winner" to determine the applied styles.

Resetting colors
Even better than lowering specificity is using using a single selector to apply styles to each element. This way your module styles never have to fight with your sidebar or site-wide styles.

Location dependence
> With no styles scoped to a single layout, we don't have to worry about what happens to the calendar when we move it from the sidebar to the main section.

Multiple inheritance
> With each of the three headings getting its own unique class, we are free to change any of them without fear of affecting the others. If you want to make changes across multiple selectors, look into preprocessor variables, mixins, or extends to handle that for you.

Further nesting
> Even at the calendar level, we still haven't applied a single style to our H2 elements. There's no need to override base, sidebar, or calendar header styles before styling new H2s in our calendar module.

Other Principles to Help You Along the Way

Single Responsibility Principle

Throughout my time at Red Hat, I found that a few other things helped me immensely when architecting our approach to writing CSS.

The *single responsibility principle* states that everything you create should be created for a single, focused reason. The styles you apply to a given selector should be created for a single purpose, and should do that single purpose extremely well.

This doesn't mean you should have individual classes for `padding-10`, `font-size-20`, and `color-green`. The single purpose we're talking about is not the styles that they apply, but rather where the styles are applied. Let's look at the following example:

```
<div class="calendar">
  <h2 class="primary-header">This Is a Calendar Header</h2>
</div>

<div class="blog">
  <h2 class="primary-header">This Is a Blog Header</h2>
</div>

.primary-header {
  color: red;
  font-size: 2em;
}
```

While the preceding example appears to be quite efficient, it has clearly broken our single responsibility principle. The class of `.primary-header` is being applied to more than one, unrelated element on the page. The "responsibility" of the `primary-header` is now to style both the calendar header and the blog header. This means that any change to the blog header will also affect the calendar header unless you do the following:

```
<div class="calendar">
  <h2 class="primary-header">This Is a Calendar Header</h2>
</div>

<div class="blog">
  <h2 class="primary-header">This Is a Blog Header</h2>
</div>

.primary-header {
  color: red;
  font-size: 2em;
}

.blog .primary-header {
  font-size: 2.4em;
}
```

This approach, while effective in the short term, brings us back to several of the problems we had at the beginning of the chapter. This new header style is now location dependent, has multiple inheritances, and introduces a game of "winning specificity."

A much more sustainable approach to this problem is to allow each class to have a single, focused responsibility:

```
<div class="calendar">
  <h2 class="calendar-header">This Is a Calendar Header</h2>
</div>

<div class="blog">
  <h2 class="blog-header">This Is a Blog Header</h2>
</div>

.calendar-header {
  color: red;
  font-size: 2em;
}

.blog-header {
  color: red;
```

```
  font-size: 2.4em;
}
```

While it's true that this approach can cause some duplication (declaring the color red twice), the gains in sustainability greatly outweigh any duplicated code. Not only will this additional code be a trivial increase in page weight (gzip loves repeated content), but there is no guarantee that the blog header will remain red, and enforcing the single responsibility principle throughout your project will ensure that further changes to the blog header are done with little work or possible regressions.

Single Source of Truth

The *single source of truth* approach takes the single responsibility theory to the next level in that not only is a class created for a single purpose, but also the styles applied to that class come from one single source. In a modular design, the design of any component must be determined by the component itself, and never imposed on it by a parent class. Let's take a look at this in action:

```
<div class="blog">
  <h2 class="blog-header">This Is a Blog Header</h2>
  ...
  <div class="calendar">
    <h2 class="calendar-header">This Is a Calendar Header</h2>
  </div>
</div>
/* calendar.css */
.calendar-header {
  color: red;
  font-size: 2em;
}

/* blog.css */
.blog-header {
  color: red;
  font-size: 2.4em;
}

.blog .calendar-header {
  font-size: 1.6em;
}
```

The intention of these styles is to decrease the size of the calendar header when it is inside of a blog article. From a design standpoint, that might make perfect sense, and what you end up with is a calendar component that changes appearance depending on where it is placed. This conditional styling is what I like to call a "context," and is something I use quite extensively throughout my design systems.

The main problem with this approach is that the decreased font size originates from the blog component, and not from within the calendar's *single source of truth*, the calendar component file. In this case, the *truth* is scattered across multiple component files. The problem with having multiple sources of truth is that it makes it very difficult to anticipate how a component is going to look placed on the page. To mitigate this problem, I suggest moving the contextual style into the calendar module code:

```
<div class="blog">
  <h2 class="blog-header">This Is a Blog Header</h2>
  ...
  <div class="calendar">
    <h2 class="calendar-header">This Is a Calendar Header</h2>
  </div>
</div>
/* calendar.css */
.calendar-header {
  color: red;
  font-size: 2em;
}

.blog .calendar-header {
  font-size: 1.6em;
}

/* blog.css */
.blog-header {
  color: red;
  font-size: 2.4em;
}
```

With this approach, we are still able to decrease the size of the calendar header when it is inside of a blog article, but by placing all of the calendar-header contextual styles into the calendar file, we can see all of the possible variations of the calendar header in a single location. This makes updating the calendar module easier (as we know all of the conditions in which it might change), and allows us to create proper test coverage for each of the variations.

Component Modifiers

While the single source of truth approach does improve clarity by placing the context inside of the component file, it can become difficult to keep track of several different contexts. If you find that the calendar header is smaller inside of dozens of different contexts, it might be time to switch from contextual modifiers to modifier classes.

Component modifiers (also called *skins* or *subcomponents*, depending on the methodology you subscribe to) allow you to create multiple variations of a component to be used in various circumstances. They work in a very similar way to contexts, but the qualifying class is part of the component rather than a parent of the component:

```
<div class="blog">
  <h2 class="blog-header">This Is a Blog Header</h2>
  ...
  <div class="calendar calendar--nested">
    <h2 class="calendar-header">This Is a Calendar Header</h2>
  </div>
</div>
/* calendar.css */
.calendar-header {
  color: red;
  font-size: 2em;
}

.calendar--nested .calendar-header {
  font-size: 1.6em;
}
/* blog.css */
.blog-header {
  color: red;
  font-size: 2.4em;
}
```

In the preceding example, we have created a `calendar--nested` modifier using the traditional BEM syntax. This class by itself does nothing, but when it is applied to the calendar component, the elements inside of the component can use it as a local context and change their appearance.

With this approach, we can use this modified calendar skin whenever we want, and we will get that smaller header (along with other changes if we want). This keeps all of your component variations in a single file, and allows you to use them (or not use them) whenever you need, not making them dependent on some random parent class.

Conclusion

This chapter covered just a small sample of the different CSS techniques that you might use to create a maintainable codebase, including the following:

- Separating container from content
- Defining roles and responsibilities of layouts versus components
- Using single, flat selectors on all of your markup
- Using other principles, such as the single responsibility principle, single source of truth, and content modifiers

The suggestions outlined here and in the previous chapter could benefit projects of any shape or size, but it is ultimately up to you and your team to decide how you are going to write your CSS. The only requirement I have is that you have these conversations, that you set expectations, and that you hold one another accountable during code review. If you do this, you will have cemented the code pillar of your frontend architecture and set your team up for success.

CHAPTER 6

JavaScript

While many would argue that JavaScript should not be a required part of our web technology stack, it is nonetheless an integral part of many of the websites we build today. Whether you are building a small portfolio site, a corporate customer portal, or a shopping website, there will inevitably be a time where you are asked to build something that can't be done with HTML and CSS alone. This might be a carousel and an image light box, or it might be a full client-side application.

This book is primarily focused on creating scalable and sustainable design systems, so I will focus on helping you plan your project and identifying quality code. I'll leave the "how to create a <insert random noun>.js–based web application" to the many other books that cover those topics. Actually, while we're talking about web applications, let's first take a moment to cover the important topic of selecting the perfect framework.

Selecting Frameworks

The first thing to get out of the way is that there is no single, perfect JavaScript framework. This chapter is not going to give you a quick answer to whether you should be using AngularJS or ReactJS. I won't even try to list all of the available options, because by the time this book is printed, the list will be full of deprecated projects, and no doubt missing the newest, hottest frameworks.

What I can tell you is this: it's very possible that you don't actually need a framework at all. Instead of focusing on which frameworks and plug-ins to use, you first need to determine which tools are necessary to achieve your goals.

This applies not only to JavaScript frameworks, but to CMS, MVC, and CSS frameworks as well. There are many successful websites that are nothing more than a static site generator, a small set of hand-crafted Sass files, and a few dozen JavaScript functions.

Start with the assumption that you aren't using Drupal or Word-Press, that you don't need AngularJS or ReactJS, and that you can write all of your own styles by hand. Then take a look at the project requirements and see how far you can get through them before you realize you need user authentication and page versioning, or that you will be handling large data sets delivered via an API. When you come up against a requirement that would be difficult to do by hand, and that has already been solved by some open source project or software, then start evaluating third-party tools.

Instead of starting off your project with a large suite of tools and a sizable starting page weight, consider simplicity and leanness as an asset. Don't give that asset up unless the benefits outweigh the added complexity and weight.

Maintaining Clean JavaScript

If you typically work on simpler projects with nothing more complicated than jQuery and a few plug-ins, you can still benefit from creating some standards around how JavaScript is written. Without some sort of expectations, you'll find that your *scripts.js* file will balloon out of control, and code will be difficult to test or refactor in the future. The following sections outline a few rules you can institute as a frontend architect to set a good baseline for JavaScript code reviews.

Keeping Your Code Clean

Unlike HTML and CSS, JavaScript is a scripting language. If you forget to close an HTML tag or write invalid CSS, the worst that can happen is a few small defects on your page. If you add too many commas or forget to close a brace in JavaScript, you have the potential of breaking your entire site.

Due to the critical nature of writing proper JavaScript, it is best practice to implement some type of linting/hinting tool along with whatever unit tests you have in your application. Including one of these tools in your workflow will not only let you catch code that could break your application, but it can also help you enforce rules about how the code is formatted, or even how it is written.

JS Hint (*http://jshint.com/*) is a great example of one of these tools. It can be used inside of your text editor, flagging errors as soon as you make them. It can even be set up inside of your build system in a way where your tests would fail if you had any code violations.

Here is a short list of some of the things JS Hint can check for you:

- Enforce the use of === and !== over == and !=
- Limit the number of nested blocks
- Limit the number of parameters a function can have
- Issue a warning if you define a function that has already been defined
- Issue a warning if you create a variable that never gets used

Create Reusable Functions

Due to the way we write jQuery, our code often starts with a CSS selector (the noun), and is followed by a string of functions (the verbs). This is just how our brains work. We first think of the thing we need to target, and then we consider what we need to do to it. Although this makes for human-readable code, it doesn't create very reusable code. Consider these contrived alert classes we're making for our CMS:

```
$('.red-alert')
    .css('background-color', "red")
    .on('click', function() {
    console.log($(this).html());
});

$('.yellow-alert')
    .css('background-color', "yellow")
    .on('click', function() {
    console.log($(this).html());
});
```

The code is short and easy to read, it's true. We know that .red-alert puts a red background on the element and then binds a click function that will print the contents of the element to the console.

We also know that our .yellow-alert creates a yellow background, and that it provides the same on-click functionality.

This might work fine for two classes, but nothing we have written here is reusable. If we ever want to create more alert colors, we'll need to duplicate one of them and then change the class and color. Even worse, if we've created a dozen of these for some reason, and we want to go back and tweak the on-click function, or add a change to the text color to go with the background, we'll have to make those updates dozens of times.

Instead of trying to write our code like a series of sentences, we create a much better system by breaking our code up into small, reusable functions. Consider the following alternative:

```
$.fn.log_text_on_click = function() {
  this.on('click', function() {
    console.log($(this).html());
  });
  return this;
};

$.fn.add_background = function(color) {
  this.css('background-color', color);
  return this;
}

$('.red-alert').add_background("red").log_text_on_click();
$('.yellow-alert').add_background("yellow").log_text_on_click();
```

Although it requires writing a few more lines of code, consider the advantages of this approach:

- We now have functions that clearly describe what they do
- If we need to create .green-alert, then we could use our pre-built add_background() and log_text_on_click() functions
- If we needed to change console.log($(this).html()); to con sole.log($(this).text()); we could do it in a single place instead of across a dozen functions
- We can use these two functions for other purposes throughout our project

Just like Sass mixins give us benefits over raw CSS, breaking your code out into reusable functions makes your code cleaner, leaner, more flexible, and more testable.

Conclusion

JavaScript is not a topic to be covered in a single chapter, but in multiple books. These tips outlined here are by no means the only ones you should consider when architecting your next project, but they are a good example of how quality code doesn't happen without some forethought. This is not to say that your developers are unable to write good code on their own, but that one developer's idea of good code will be quite different from the next, and the next. Creating a baseline of coding standards is the only way to ensure that code reviews are fair, and that developers know what is expected of them.

CHAPTER 7

Red Hat Code

The fall of 2014 saw the launch of the Redhat.com website. I'd only been on this multiyear project since the spring prior, so while I was pretty familiar with the code architecture at launch, I'd had little opportunity to shape it. The scope of the project and our looming deadline meant I spent most of my time getting the work done, and little time wondering if that work I was doing truly met the needs of the organization.

In the end, the site launched, and by all measures it was a success. The UI was efficient, the site loaded quickly, and few argued that the site wasn't attractive. But I can still recall that fateful afternoon when I was asked a very simple question: "How modular is our design? We'd like to be able to share small parts of our theme with other company websites."

It took me a little while to recover from the chuckle that welled up inside of me. You see, being intimately familiar with the markup, JavaScript, and CSS written for this project, I knew that this design was the antithesis of modular! We did a lot of great work on this theme, but creating a modular design was never even a consideration.

Dependency Bloat

If someone were looking to render a single band of content with our styles, they would first need to load the following:

Bootstrap CSS: 114 KB (uncompressed)

This site didn't leverage too much of the Bootstrap library, but all of the CSS was written with the assumption that Bootstrap had already washed all over it. Pull those styles out, and the page becomes completely broken.

Core Site CSS: 500 KB

Though each band of content typically had a single file associated with it, the styles from that single file were never the *single source of truth* for that band. Styles cascaded in from several different locations and were often overridden based on location or page class.

Location-Dependent Nightmare

The markup approach that the project used was to style from the band down. We had several types of bands, and most of the styles were scoped to and repeated inside of that band class. Here is an extreme example of an H3 inside of a hero band:

```
.about-contact .hero1 .container >
section.features-quarter >
section.f-contact h3
```

Not only is this style scoped to a single page (`about-contact`), but we need to make sure that the `features-quarter` section is the direct descendant of the container class so that we aren't accidentally styling descendants of the wrong section element! This top-down styles approach meant that every change we did required longer and longer, more specific selectors. It also meant that none of the contents of a band could be easily rearranged or replaced, as the markup order was incredibly strict.

Sure, we could pull out a single band and consolidate all of the required styles into a single file, but doing so would basically mean completely re-creating the component Sass partial from scratch, and we'd still have a problem with trying to make the markup modular.

So, when I was asked about how modular our design was, and if we could start sharing out styles to other departments, there was only one thing that I could say. I said that we'd have to completely rewrite the markup and the CSS for anything we wanted to share, and while we were at it, we should update the markup on our site as well.

I was quite certain that such a drastic departure from our current design approach would have me laughed right out of the room. Therefore you can understand my surprise when they not only said "yes," but we were given several weeks to work out the new system while the newly launched site was in code freeze. So here we had a fully fleshed-out design, a very capable development team, and carte blanche to create a modular, scalable, and sustainable design system that could be deployed into a live, highly trafficked, high-profile site as we built it. All I could think was, when can we start?!

Breaking the Design Down

As I said before, the original approach we took was to design from the top of the band down. The appearance of the contents and the way that it was laid out were completely determined by the type of band we were using. We had logo walls, a hero band, testimonials bands, blog teaser bands—you name it. Each of those bands had its own Sass partial, and all of the styles were scoped under the band name.

In a way, this worked well. You usually knew where to go to update a given band's styles. But the problem was that we had to continually create more bands every time we needed to support a new design or layout. We might have had a well-established visual language, but that had never been translated into a design system that could be used to create new patterns.

So the first task we undertook was breaking the design down into its smallest possible pieces. We knew that once we had the building blocks of this design system, we could create anything that the visual language needed to communicate. The first step was to look at our designs and break them down into repeatable layout patterns.

As we took a look at several of our most common band types, we noticed that most of them shared a number of common layout patterns (see Figure 7-1). We had content with a sidebar, content in equally sized columns, galleries of images or icons that spanned five per row, and black and white cards that held their content inside a bit of padding and a background.

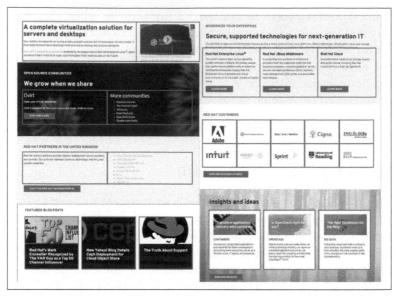

Figure 7-1. The various layouts of our design system

We quickly realized that if we created a method for reusing these few simple layout concepts, we could create the layout for every single band in our entire website. We wouldn't need a logo wall band with a specified layout, and an insights band with a different layout. We could create a single band that had many layout options. We could also create card layouts that did nothing more than apply padding and a black or white background for the contents inside of them.

Cataloging Components

In the same way that we broke out all our various layouts, we started taking a look at the contents of each of these layouts and realized we could reproduce a majority of them with just a small handful of components.

A component, as compared to a layout, describes the visual appearance of a small piece of content. Components are meant to be dumb and flexible. They have zero opinion about their backgrounds, their widths, or their external padding and margins.

The power of this relationship between layouts and components is evidenced by the fact that you can drop any three components into a three-column layout and it'll look like they were meant to go there, all without a single extra bit of code. Each component will fill the entire width of the column it was placed in, and the first line of the block quote will be level with first line of the blog entry, which will line up with the image in the third column (see Figure 7-2).

Figure 7-2. No component has top margins, so three different components will all line up

Once we realized that this powerful system was based on a few simple, yet highly important, rules and relationships, we set out to codify them into a more official form. We wanted to make sure that as we introduced new layouts and components to the system, each merge request would conform to a series of rules. We called these our Road Runner Rules.

The Road Runner Rules

Just prior to our contemplating these new rules, my Twitter stream had been bombarded by a story about Chuck Jones and a list of nine rules that he'd purportedly written for the writers and animators of the *Road Runner* cartoon. This list set forth the rules under which the entire *Road Runner* universe was meant to run. Rules like "The road runner cannot harm the coyote, except by going 'beep beep'" and "No dialog, ever, except 'beep beep'" helped guide the animators and writters of each cartoon to create a consistent and cohesive universe.

Whether the story was authentic or not, it was this consistent and cohesive universe that I wanted to create for my own team. I knew that the only way we could avoid writing a swift road-runner kick to the coyote's jaw, followed by a fowl cry of "can't catch me, sucker!" would be to distill the rules that govern our design system into a small, palatable list of Road Runner Rules.

Writing Your Own Rules

When I came up to write my list of Road Runner Rules, I started with almost twice as many rules as we have now. As I got into the double digits, I found that with each rule I wrote, I would think of two or three more.

With the thought of making a set of rules old enough to buy me a drink, I realized that I wasn't making rules anymore, but rather I was writing the documentation for our entire system. And the problem with *that* was that I already had written our documentation!

I didn't need to describe how the coyote would order products from an Acme catalog and that they would show up seconds later in his mailbox, only to be his ultimate downfall. I needed to enforce that "no outside force [could] harm the coyote," except for his ineptitude or the failure of those Acme products.

What I needed was a small set of immutable rules, not a fully developed set of instructions. Apparently what I needed were some rules for my rules!

Now I know you're probably thinking that this is either excessively meta or an exercise in absurdity. But just like a good-looking style guide has its unique design and rules, and a solidly written data schema is written to the spec of its parent schema, our Road Runner Rules needed to be written with their own set of governing rules.

These are the rules we eventually came up with:

- Only include immutable rules, not general instructions
- Always boil each rule down to its simplest expression
- Always state the rule first, then explain "If not, then what?"
- Every rule should include one of the following: *always, never, only, every, don't,* or *do*

These rules would help us avoid writing general instructions containing several sentences that never actually got to the point. Astute readers will also note that all four of these rules conform to the Road Runner Rules as well.

So revision after revision, our team reworded, rewrote, and deleted items off the list until our design system had the following list of rules:

- A layout never imposes padding or element styles on its children. It is only concerned with their horizontal or vertical alignment and spacing.

- Themes and other data attributes never force changes in appearance; they are always a context that layouts, components, and elements can subscribe to.

- A component always touches all four sides of its parent container. No element will have top or left margins, and all last children (right or bottom) will have their margins cleared.

- The component itself never has backgrounds, widths, floats, padding, or margins. Component styles only target the elements inside.

- Every element has a single, unique, component-scoped class. All styles are applied directly to that selector, modified only by contexts and themes.

- Elements never use top margins. The first element touches the top of its component.

- JavaScript is never bound to any element class. Functionality is "opted in" via data attributes.

These rules cover not only the specific relationship between layout and component, but also other areas of the design system including themes, elements, and JavaScript. Let's dive into some of the more interesting decisions we made regarding our approach to HTML and CSS.

A Single Selector for Everything

I've spent too much of my life creating generic, universal classes that could be applied to any element, only to realize how difficult they were to maintain as the project grew. Because the classes were universal and could be used on just about anything, it was often easier to create a new class than it was to update the original one. Therefore, one of the things I was most determined to do was create single, unique, flat classes for every element. You can read a bunch more about this by revisiting Chapter 6, but this principle was a key part of fulfilling the needs of the rule that requires every element to have a single, unique, component-scoped class.

Single Responsibility Principle

In some circles, the single responsibility principle, applied to CSS, means that each class has a small, focused responsibility, and that one class will set the box model properties of an element, while another sets the typography, and a third sets the color and background.

For our system and set of rules, the single responsibility principle means that every class I create is made to be used for a single purpose, in a single place. Therefore, if I make a change to .rh-standard-band-title, I can be confident that the only effect this will have on our site is to change the appearance of the title inside of the rh-standard-band.

This also means that if we decide to deprecate rh-standard-band, we can completely remove all of the associated CSS without fear of breaking some other component that "hijacked inheritance" and became reliant on that CSS. It's because of this desire to not "use and abuse the cascade" (*http://bit.ly/abuse-cascade*) that I made sure that every class is used only for the single purpose for which it was created (Figure 7-3).

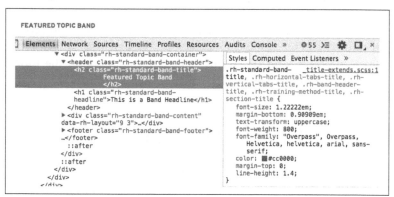

Figure 7-3. Each class is created for a single purpose

Single Source of Truth

Once we have a page full of single-classed elements we can be pretty confident that our changes to .rh-standard-band-title won't affect any other part of the system, but what is to say that our .rh-standard-band-title can't be affected by something else? This is why it is so important to maintain a single source of truth for every component, and by extension, every element on the page. This means not relying on any H2 styles, or "header H2," or any other selector outside of the Standard Band Sass file to style this element.

This is not to say that our title can never be altered or modified by an outside force. What this does mean is that anything that these modifiers or contexts do to an element will be defined in the same place as the element's original styles, not in some other location. So while I have no objections to `.some-context .rh-standard-band-title`, these styles will always be defined in the Standard Band Sass partial, and never anywhere else.

Opt-in Modifiers

As I already mentioned, I have no objections to having modifiers on my components, but in every single instance these modifications need to be opt-in. What this means is that if I define Modifier A for Component B, then Modifier A would have no effect on any Component C unless it opted in to that modifier.

Before we dive into an example, let me explain one architectural choice I made in regards to modifiers and contexts. While BEM, SMACSS, and OOCSS all have conventions for modifiers, themes, or skins, they all require adding modifying classes to the block or element. I decided to take a different approach that wouldn't require any additional classes. I was really determined to, as Ben Frain (*http://bit.ly/rwd-frain*) puts it, "let the thing be the thing." I never wanted anyone to confuse the "thing's" class and its modifier. So I decided that all modifiers and contexts would be put inside data attributes instead, like this:

```
<div class="foo" data-bar="baz">...</div>
```

This separation had another benefit beyond distinguishing purpose and role. Classes are very one-dimensional: either the class is present or it is not. A data attribute, on the other hand, is two-dimensional, having the attribute itself and the value passed into it. To compensate for the missing dimension, you'll often find classes using a namespace to define which group they belong to. A data attribute has an explicit namespace, and can therefore pass any necessary value into it. It may be a few more characters, but using data attributes makes it really obvious that our component has a property of `data-align` and that it can be set to a variety of values.

OK, now back to that example.

The `rh-card--layout` is a layout tool that we use to wrap content inside of padding and a background. This card (Figure 7-4) has a black background because we've stated that `data-rh-theme="dark"` sets a black background on the card within our card Sass partial. In the same way, we've defined that `data-rh-justify="center"` will center all of the content in the card.

Figure 7-4. A basic card with a black background and a dark theme

```scss
<!-- card.scss -->
.rh-card--layout {
  padding: 30px;
  &[data-rh-theme="light"]{
    background: white;
  }
  &[data-rh-theme="dark"]{
    background: black;
  }
  &[data-rh-justify="center"]{
    ...
  }
  &[data-rh-justify="top"]{
    ...
  }
  &[data-rh-justify="justify"]{
    ...
```

```
    }
  }
```

Along with center we've also specified other justify values, including top and justify (Figure 7-5).

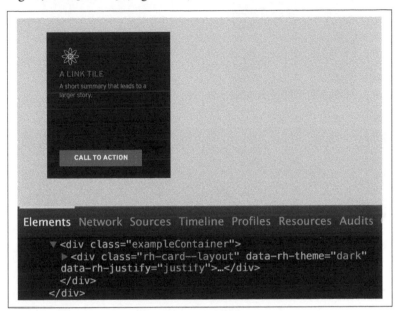

Figure 7-5. A card with vertically justified content

So with a single switch in a data attribute, we can switch the appearance of this card based on values specific to the card's Sass partial.

Now one thing that we have not defined in the card Sass partial is alignment. We typically leave left/right/center alignment as an option for individual components using data-rh-align, so we've intentionally chosen to not opt in to that property. This means that no matter what modifiers other components or layouts might use, they will have zero effect if applied to the card (see Figure 7-6).

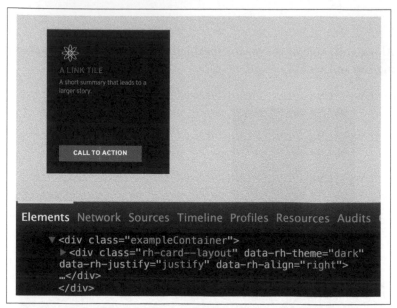

Figure 7-6. The card is not affected by properties not explicitly prescribed

Opt-in Context

One of the mantras of our design system is that a component should look the same regardless of where you place it. But just as we want our components to be resilient and predictable, we also want them to be smart and flexible. This is the reason that we came up with context styles.

A context style means that a component can define the way it behaves when it is inside of some other parent element, or when that parent has a specific data attribute. Again, we aren't setting all H2s in our sidebar to be green, but if we had a `.widget-title` that needed to be green when it was inside the sidebar, we could do that! Let's look at our card example again.

Inside of the card, our `data-rh-theme` property actually acts as a modifier and a context. It's a modifier in that it changes the card background from black to white (Figure 7-7), but it is also a context for the elements inside of it.

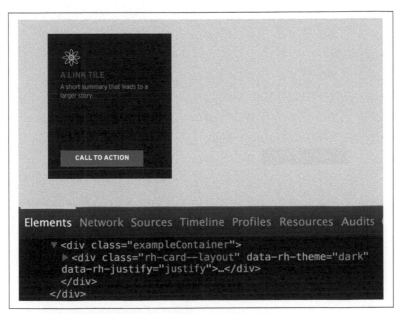

Figure 7-7. This dark theme card has a white icon

When we switch from the dark to the light theme, you can see that not only does the background change color (the modifier), but the icon changes color as well from white to black (Figure 7-8). Now I'm not saying that our new theme is forcing all of the child text elements to change color (the title and button didn't change at all). This is an opt-in style on the icon, written right inside of the link-tile Sass file (Figure 7-9).

These opt-in contexts allow us to create variations for any component without affecting the original component. They provide controlled variation, scoped to the component classes, defined solely inside of the component Sass partial.

This does mean doing a little bit of repetitive work if we want the same modifier or context to affect multiple components. But I have never regretted this decision as our system grew. Not only have we made it easier to reuse modifiers and contexts through mixins and extends, but having a finite number of component variations helps us avoid hard-to-find bugs and improves our ability to create comprehensive visual regression coverage. Because all modifiers and contexts are defined in the Sass partial, we can look at any component and know without a doubt all of its possible visual variations.

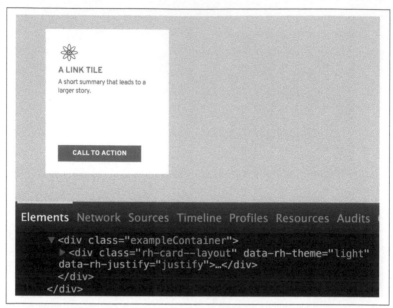

Figure 7-8. This light theme card has a black icon

```
[data-rh-theme~="dark"]
.rh-link-tile-icon {
    color: ■white;
}
```

Figure 7-9. The icon subscribes to the dark context to turn white

```
[data-rh-theme~="light"]
.rh-link-tile-icon {
    color: □#252527;
}
```

Figure 7-10. The icon subscribes to the light context to turn black

Semantic Grids

With a solid foundation for our components, the next thing we needed to do was figure out how to combine them together into different layouts. In the past, when we were less modular, we wrote styles for each unique band, including the band layout. When we had a band full of logos, we gave the band a class name and then explicitly applied a layout to that band. The problem with this approach is that nothing, other than the entire band, was reusable. If we had another band that used the same layout but different content, we'd need to create an entirely new band, along with styles for the layout.

So now that we'd broken down our logo wall to a collection of images, buttons, and headers, we needed similarly modular layouts that can be reused any time we wanted. What this meant was that we needed to put the layout back into the DOM, something we had fought so hard against when moving away from bootstrap grid.

Fortunately, there is middle ground between the bootstrap grids of old with their containers, rows, and column containers, and applying unique layouts to the `.logo-wall` band, and every other new combination of content that needed layout.

Our solution was to create a collection of common grid patterns that could be applied to a layout via a data attribute (Figure 7-11). With the attribute set on the parent element, all of the child elements would fall into whatever grid type they were placed into. This allowed us to keep our separation between layouts and components, while still providing a solution for setting our grid in the markup.

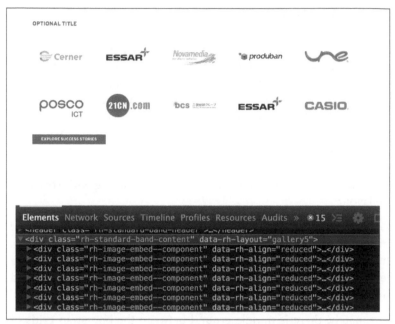

Figure 7-11. A single data attribute allows us to set the layout on a large group of images

In the preceding example, you can see that we are applying a `data-rh-layout` attribute to the band content region (one of the band's major content areas). This attribute once again shows how data attributes are great at organizing numerous context values. With this single attribute we can pass in dozens of different layouts, each used to set the widths and margins of the contained components.

In this case, with `gallery5` passed in, the CSS is applying roughly a 20% width to all of its child elements. By placing all of the grid information in the parent element, we are able to drop any combination of components into the content region without ever adding a class, or wrapping it in some row or column container. So when we want to change this logo wall from a five-column to a four-column layout, the only thing we need to do is change a single attribute on the parent element (Figure 7-12).

Figure 7-12. By changing a single data attribute we can change the layout of these logos

With a single attribute change, we have modified the entire layout of the band. We didn't have to write new CSS (modular) and we didn't have to apply classes to the content (semantic). It's a win-win! Now we have an inventory of galleries and common layout combinations of our 12-column grid (6 6, 3 9, 4 4 4, etc). These layouts cover 99% of the content we need to create. If we find that we need something more unique, we can create a custom grid layout, document it, and make it available for anyone to apply to their content.

Now that we have a set of modular and customizable containers that can house our components and apply layouts to them, we can start building our logo walls, featured events, blog teasers, and every other band our site requires.

PART III

The Process Pillar

The process pillar was created in order to define the steps required to get code from the developer's brain to the user's browser. It encompasses each permutation the code goes through, from qualified idea to validated design to accepted commit to deployed code.

If you've been doing development for long enough, you'll probably notice that our processes have evolved immensely in the past several years. My first experience in web development involved being asked to digest two months' worth of email correspondence, determine what the client was asking for, and then FTP into their server and make the necessary changes.

This, in hindsight, was a horrible way to perform updates to a website. What would have happened if I misread the email and changed the wrong thing? What if I had accidentally deleted a large chunk of CSS, inadvertently breaking other pages on the site? What would have happened if I fixed a JavaScript bug, but it introduced two other bugs? Now, by itself, these problems would be annoying, and a prime example of why you never use FTP to edit the live site! But what happens if you aren't backing up often enough, and you are left with a broken website to fix, and you still have a list of tasks to complete?

Fortunately, for most of us, we've learned from these mistakes and are following much better practices these days. Instead of FTPing changes sent in an email, we now:

1. Use issue tracking and user stories to properly track workflows and mark completed tasks
2. Set up development environments where you can properly test code changes
3. Create build processes that compile, validate, and test code
4. Get feedback from story owners before any code is accepted
5. Push the committed code to a central code repository
6. Employ a build system that seamlessly pushes out the new batch of code into production, and could roll that patch back, restoring original functionality if needed

Are You Up for the Task?

As a frontend architect you will usually be tasked with developing, or at least championing, each of the steps just listed. Any weak links in this process will quickly surface as a pain point for developers, or a source of constant unmet expectations or regressions.

As I've said in previous chapters, when it comes to frontend architecture, the "user" is the developer. The tools we select, the code we write, and the processes we create are all aimed at allowing the developer to write the most efficient, error-free, scalable, and sustainable design system possible.

In this part, we will look at the larger picture of onboarding and equipping new developers. We'll dive into the process they go through to turn requirements into published code. Then we will dive right into the heart of the process in discussing the role of task runners and how they help us to create better code in less time.

CHAPTER 8

Workflow

At the heart of the process pillar is the workflow. The workflow is how ideas are turned into reality; or less altruistically, how bugs are squashed and features added. The frontend workflow does not exist in a vacuum, though, so it is always important to look at it in context of the whole team, and then to break it down from there.

The Old Development Workflow

I'm sure I've already complained about this a few times, but it bears repeating. Don't use the diagram shown in Figure 8-1 for your web development workflow. The days of taking a bunch of markup and making it match a PSD file are done, over, dead, and hopefully buried where no one will ever find them again. Frontend development can no longer be putting a nice coat of paint on a mess of HTML; we aren't here to simply pretty things up.

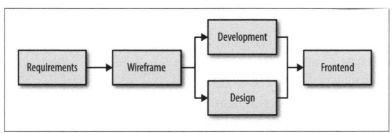

Figure 8-1. The old development workflow

The New Development Workflow

In stark contrast to the previous workflow, which focused on water-fall handoffs from product owner to UX to development and design to frontend developer, our modern workflow is something completely different. In order to create performant, responsive, accessible websites, we will have to turn this old workflow model on its head. When we do, we get something like the workflow depicted in Figure 8-2.

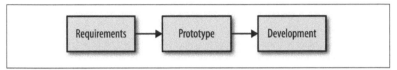

Figure 8-2. The new development workflow

Requirements

We always need to start with gathering requirements. It's how we define our need and quantify our success. The key difference in our new workflow is the audience of those requirements: UX, design, development, *and* frontend development. This group of mixed disciplines means that our new requirements will be focused on creating an entire in-browser solution, rather than a wireframe approximation or a static comp.

By having all four disciplines interacting with requirement gathering, we are able to spot holes or incongruities in requirements much sooner. Too often, problems with source order, performance-crippling designs, or broken user experience aren't discovered until development is done and deadlines are fast approaching.

Prototyping

Instead of passing large artifacts from person to person, our new workflow focuses on iterating through user experience models, visual designs, and frontend solutions.

Prototypes provide a common space for discussion and feedback. They put fully fleshed-out ideas into both desktop and mobile browsers. This is the place where ideas can be formed, tossed out, revived, polished. Once developers and product owners are satisfied with the work, they can also be accepted.

It's not until this point of acceptance that we move our prototype (which has the advantage of being cheap to make and highly flexible) into development (which is costly to produce and inherently inflexible).

Development

At this point, our feature is in an amazing position to succeed. Not only are we staring off with a thoroughly tested design, but we have all of the markup necessary to achieve it as well. The developer's job becomes collecting and processing data from the database, and then passing it through to the specified markup. Developers will rarely need to go back and add an extra class, remove a container div, or change the source order, because all of that iteration and testing has already occurred.

If you are building your product in a way that the prototype and website share CSS and JS, developers should finish their work with a fully functional, fully styled, interactive, responsive, vetted, and approved product. This not only helps the developers, but it is also a boon to the quality assurance team. Instead of referencing old, possibly out-of-date, requirement documents and trying to determine if the developer's work is correct, QA is able to compare their work line by line with the gold standard: the prototype.

Frontend Workflow

Moving from the macro to the micro, let's look at the importance of a good prototyping process and ensuring that your team's frontend developers are all set up to succeed. Many of these topics are cross discipline, but all of them have a profound impact on the productivity and happiness of your frontend developers.

Now, we can't make any assumptions about what our developers know or are already equipped with, so our frontend workflow starts as soon as a new developer is hired. It is important to understand all of the steps required for a new developer, sitting down in front of code for the first time, with a new laptop, to write their first line of quality code.

Provisioning

The first step for any new developer is to install the necessary software and create the required setup for your code environment. This typically involves installing and setting up your favorite code editors, installing a few Adobe products, and downloading your favorite browsers. Once software is up and running, there are usually several steps to setting up Git and server access. Lastly, your new developers will be trying to sort out the hundreds of various web services and passwords.

Yes, this might seem a bit mundane, but the more streamlined this process can be, the quicker they can move on to actually working on your code.

Spinning Up Local

Interacting with version control will usually be the first thing a developer does when they start the day, and the last thing they'll do when they're done. It is the tool that gives them access to your website's code and allows them to push new code once they are done. At this point, they'll probably be cloning your code to their local environment and setting it up to run on their own machine. This can be as simple as:

```
git clone <repo> && cd <repo-name> && make website
```

or it can be a long process of pulling down multiple repos, setting up a local database, configuring various server settings, or even modifying computer networking or VPN setup. Whatever your process is, make sure it is spelled out clearly in the *README.md* file and gives resources and people to contact if they have questions about specific steps.

Don't underestimate the time this process can take! I've been on projects where this setup only takes a few minutes, and I've heard war stories where it took several weeks before a new developer could actually get the site running locally.

So now our developer has a code editor, a browser, and a local site that they can edit. What else could they ever need before they start working? How about something to work on? Let's talk about that next.

Story Writing

Whether you call them tasks, tickets, stories, or jobs, there is a communicational need to distill a human's thoughts and desires into a focused, actionable, and testable request. It'd be great if we could just read everyone's minds, but short of that we are writing user stories that describe in great detail the problem, the proposed solution, and the requirements that must be met before that story is complete.

This need to define everything into bite-sized requests is no different in frontend development. As we move away from building pages and into building design systems, we need to make sure that the way we slice up our work reflects our new approach. What this means is that we need to stop writing stories such as "update the 'about us' page." These requests typically involve dozens of small typographical and layout changes, and might include a request like "double the padding on the call to action (CTA) button." Here are the many reasons why this story is so bad:

- Are we being asked to change the padding on all of the CTAs or just the one on the "about us" page?
- If we aren't updating all of the CTAs, are there other pages other than "about us" that need to use this larger button?
- Is the person who wrote this task even allowed to make site-wide changes? What happens if we change all of the CTAs and the person writing tasks for the homepage doesn't want this new button?
- What happens if one person is updating the CTA on the "about us" page, and someone else has a task directing them to change the CTA on the "contact us" page?
- Why is a simple change to the global CTA button being grouped together with dozens of other local and global changes?

Instead of stories to make several changes to a single page, we should be focusing our frontend development stories on what changes we are actually making to our system. Rather than a large story with dozens of changes, we should have a story that looks like this: "Create a new CTA button that has 16px of padding instead of 8px of padding for use on any internal page."

This story makes it obvious that we are not updating the original CTA, but rather creating a variation. We know that this change is

100% opt-in, and will have no effect on the website until we go back to the "about us" page (a separate story) and update the HTML to use this variation.

By focusing on the components, rather than focusing on the work for a single page, we ensure that we're always thinking design system first, and how our changes will affect it. This creates a more resilient system, and helps to avoid conflicting work on multiple pages.

Development

Now that we have a story that is focused on updating the system, rather than updating a page, we can proceed in making this contrived, and arguably minimal, change to the design system. We've got a button that typically has 8px of padding, and we need to make a variation that has 16px of padding. Let's take a look at the code we'll be making changes to:

```
.cta {
    background: blue;
    color: white;
    padding: 8px;
}
```

Before our new developer dives into writing some new CSS, let's have them follow a common and well-accepted practice of creating a feature branch. A feature branch is a Git branch that forks off of your main development branch, and lets you develop and commit code with the intent of eventually merging the feature back into the main branch. The advantage of this approach is that you don't commit incomplete code to the master branch. You are committing the code in a place where others can check it out and test it before merging it back into your main branch.

With a new feature branch created, it's now time for the developer to write some CSS! There's only one problem: there are a ton of ways that our developer could write this CSS.

They could create a completely new button to replace the old one:

```
.cta-large {
    background: blue;
    color: white;
    padding: 16px;
}
```

If they are using Sass, they might end up creating a mixin to handle this work and refactor both buttons:

```
@mixin button($size) {
  background: blue;
  color: white;
  padding: $size;

}

.cta {
@include button(8px);
}

.cta-large {
@include button(8px);
}
```

They could opt to create a button modifier so our button would include both .cta and .cta-large:

```
.cta-large {
  padding: 16px;
}

/* Example HTML would be <a class="cta cta-large">
```

Or they could use data attributes instead of classes and write:

```
.cta[data-size="large"] {
  padding: 16px;
}

/* Example HTML would be <a class="cta" data-size="large">
```

It should be pretty apparent that even something as simple as creating a new button variation could be accomplished through a number of different approaches. And even though all four of these approaches accomplish the same goal, they each have significantly different effects on the design system that we're trying to create and maintain.

This is exactly why we spent so much time during the code pillar stage defining the way that we write our selectors, write our CSS, and create element variations. With documentation available to describe our coding practices, the developer will have a guide to creating the correct code and push that new code up to their feature branch.

At this point, the dev's feature branch is ready for review and they can create a merge request (or pull request) that is equivalent to saying "I've got some code that I feel is complete. Can you please review it, then merge it into the main branch?" This takes a bit more time than just merging the code directly into master, but this pull request creates an opportunity for review and feedback to the developer before the code is accepted.

Sometimes this review process discovers a major flaw in the code, or determines that it is not in line with design system expectations. Sometimes the review just provides an opportunity to suggest better ways to write the CSS, optimizations to the Sass functions, or improved clarity to the documentation. Even if the merge just gets a big :thumbsup:, having a second eye on a change to the design system helps to ensure that the code contribution is the best contribution that it could be.

So, now that our developer's code has been merged into the main branch, it's time to get this code into production.

Distribution

Our developer has done it! They have written a patch to our current codebase that solved our CTA problem, and after some code review and quality assurance, we are ready to get these changes out to our users. In this case, let's assume that we chose to create a Sass mixin to create both a .cta button and a .cta-large button. These changes to our Sass files are now committed to master, but that does not guarantee the new CSS has found its way to the live website where users can use it. Before you fire up your FTP client, let's consider some of the pros and cons of various distribution methods.

Committing Compiled Assets

It is best practice in any version control system to commit only the bare essentials of your code. This means, for example, we tell Git to ignore our temporary files, or any assets that need to download to compile our code (we'll talk much more about this next chapter). The rationale behind this is that our website doesn't need those temp files or node modules to perform properly. These files also significantly add to the file size of our project, and they will end up being a constant source of conflicts, as your local temp files might not match up with the ones last committed.

Unfortunately, there is one file type that sits right between "essential to the functionality of the website" and "source of bloat and constant conflicts": our compiled assets. Any time we compile Sass, Coffee-Script, or LESS; add vendor prefixes with post processors; concatenate some JavaScript files; create an icon font; or process our images to reduce file size, we are creating compiled assets. What are we supposed to do with all of these files? What happens if we commit them? Is it possible to avoid committing them and still have a functioning website?

In many cases, you will find yourself forced to commit these assets. It's not ideal, but unless you want to ditch your preprocessor and write that CSS file by hand, you might just need to add it to the repo. The advantage of this approach is that your repo always has all of the files required to render properly. If your servers are set up to fetch files directly from the GitHub master branch, you'll have everything you need to display your website. Another benefit is that if nontechnical users pull down a copy of the site, they can view it without having to go through the lengthy process of setting up the compile tools.

Of course, for this small advantage, we also get to deal with a host of other problems, the greatest of them being merge conflicts. If you've ever tried to perform a Git rebase on a project that has compiled assets committed, you'll know what I'm talking about. Even beyond rebasing, whenever you merge two branches with compiled code, you most likely will be dealing with merge conflicts in those compiled assets. Now, resolving those conflicts is easy (compile everything again and commit that), but this means that you'll never have a merge request where your frontend devs aren't pulled in to resolve some merge conflict in the outputted CSS.

If you are hoping to avoid these problems and keep compiled assets out of your codebase, you've got a few possible options. Let's take a look.

Continuous Integration Server

Using a service like Jenkins or Travis CI will provide benefits far beyond the scope of this book, but one of their many uses is to perform operations on our codebase before pushing the code to our production server. What this means is that we can omit our compiled assets from Git and our CI server will perform our compiling tasks for us between checking out our code and pushing that code to production.

This approach offers more than just the convenience of keeping our repository clean—it also helps to protect us from unexpected regressions. If we are committing compiled assets, whenever *my* feature branch is merged into master, the compiled assets in master are 100% the product of how *my* machine compiled those assets. Once another developer's feature branch gets merged in, my feature is going to be rendered with the assets compiled on that developer's computer.

Sure, other developers will be compiling using my new Sass code and JavaScript files, but there's always a possibility that differences in our operating systems or system setup or installed software could cause a difference in the compiled code. On the other hand, if we are testing our feature branches using the CI compiled code, and the CI server is compiling the assets pushed to production, we can be confident that those assets will be compiled the same way, every time.

Tagged Releases

One of the powers of Git is its ability to create tagged releases. A tag is a snapshot in a project's history, based off the code at a single commit. Tags are a convenient way to distribute your code whether you are pushing to a production server or pushing to a distribution channel (which we'll talk about next). One of the powers of a tag is that the code can be based off of any branch, not just your production branch.

Why Would You Ever Want to Do This?

One method for creating new releases of your software is to create a release branch for every version of your software. If v1.1 is coming out, you'll create a branch called v1.1-dev off of master, and you will work in that branch until the release is ready. Usually if there are bugs in the v1.1-dev branch, you'll address them in that branch, and then have the option to merge those fixes back into master. Sometimes the code fix that is required to get v1.1 out the door isn't the same code that you'd want to put back into the master branch. You might just be looking at a temporary fix and filing a ticket in the backlog to fix it properly.

One other way to take advantage of tagged releases is to only commit your compiled assets inside of those tags. Remember, tags always refer to a single commit, and persist even after the branch that created that commit is deleted. There's nothing saying that this single commit has to even get merged back into master. I'll talk about the process we use at Red Hat in Chapter 10. For now, let's finish by looking at how we can use distribution channels to get our code pushed out to not just a single server, but many servers.

Distribution Channels

If all of your production code is inside of a single repo, you're probably not worrying too much about distribution channels. But if you are creating a theme or a library or a module that is used by dozens, if not hundreds, of websites, you've probably looked into the various distribution channels available to you outside of simple version control. There are more than you might think, and you often have more than one option. Here's a short, inevitably incomplete list to at least get you started:

- NPM (Node Package Manager)
- Bower
- Ruby Gems
- Composer
- Yeoman Generators
- Drupal Contrib Modules and Drush
- WordPress Plug-ins
- Homebrew
- Sublime Text Package Control
- RPM
- PEAR

Regardless of which type of code you write (PHP, Node, Ruby, CMS module, Mac software, Unix software, VIM plug-in, IDE plug-in), you'll find that someone has written a package manager for distributing it. Considering that Bower is actually a node module, there are even package managers to manager your package managers! There are several benefits to using a package manager to distribute your code, so having more than we could ever need certainly is better than the alternative.

Package managers provide the following benefits:

Push out versioned releases
This means users of your code won't automatically be upgraded to the newest release, but instead they can evaluate any new code before upgrading.

Easy for users to know when new releases are available
Most package managers have built-in notifications and internal upgrade systems that make it easy to find upgraded modules and pull down the new code.

Distribute only the files required for the user
You'll often have a large build system creating your distributed code, and using a package manager allows you to distribute only the files that matter.

Publish code from within a private repository
Sometimes it is not possible to give everyone access to your Git repo. Private version control and firewalls often keep source code under lock and key, even if the end product is meant for general consumption. Package managers allow you to get that distributed code into a public space.

Take some time and look at the various options you have for your project. You're never locked into a single system (many projects are on Bower and NPM), but you'll want to be confident in whatever system you decide on, as your users will be creating build systems that depend on this code. So then let's talk about the build system you'll be using to create this shareable code, and the systems that rely on code published by others.

CHAPTER 9

Task Runners

For many frontend developers, Sass was our first build system, or task runner. Before Sass, our workflow was to hit Save on our CSS file and then refresh the browser. With Sass, we took our first step on the journey toward automation nirvana. Some might say that we just added one more terminal command to our workflow, but for those first discovering Sass, that small task was well worth the effort.

When we discovered Compass, we not only found a trove of CSS3 mixins that saved us from visiting CSS3 Generator (*http://css3genera tor.com/*) dozens of times a day, but we also learned about the power of a single configuration file for each project. With Compass, we could create a *config.rb* file that described the paths to important folders, specified settings for development versus production, and toggled important troubleshooting tools. This single file could be saved and shared with the rest of the team, making onboarding new developers much easier.

As the Sass community continued to grow, a large array of Compass plug-ins began to emerge, providing everything from advanced color functions to grid systems to modular scale to media query management. These tools, all distributed as gems, could be imported directly into any project with Compass.

Compass also allowed module developers to tap into the power of Ruby, accessing local files, performing Ruby functions, compiling Ruby templates, and passing the data back to the Sass file. This allowed people to write modules that used advanced math not possible in Sass alone. Compass also tapped into this functionality, allowing users to automatically generate sprite maps from folders of PNG files, or to query image files and return height and width values.

So now, with a single `compass compile` command, a developer could compile all of their Sass into a target CSS directory, while each image URL is resolved to the image folder, and font references resolved to the font folder. The Sass could be compiled using popular frameworks like Susy grids, Modular Scale, Breakpoint, and Color Schemer. It could do all of this while creating several custom image sprites and querying dozens of JPEG files to use their dimensions to set height and width properties in the CSS.

Compass was not only our first exposure to the world of build systems, but it was also the primary reason that many of us resisted moving over to a new breed of Node.js task runners that were quickly growing in popularity. After a quick introduction to tools like Grunt and Gulp, most of us (myself included) were quick to reply "Oh, just like Compass, but more complicated." For a developer whose entire build process had been managed by Compass, setting up Grunt just to compile Sass felt like a completely unnecessary step. But once we got Gulp or Grunt set up to compile Sass, we started to turn our eyes to the host of other things we could do and quickly realized that our build processes would never be the same.

Going All In with Task Runners

Embracing Node.js-based task runners had a bit of a domino effect in my workflow. As a Grunt user, not only did I now have 13,000+ modules at my disposal, but these modules provided functionality in every possible area of my workflow, not just Sass and CSS. Here is a list of some of the things I now use a task runner to do:

- Install required Ruby gems and Bower packages
- Clear out temp folders
- Create sym links
- Compile Sass
- Concatenate JavaScript
- Load third-party JavaScript libraries
- Compile Icon-font from SVGs
- Process images, reducing file size, cropping to multiple sizes
- Rsync files to remove server
- Create Git tags

- Run visual regression tests
- Compile the style guide
- Autoprefix vendor prefixes
- Compile component library
- Lint my Sass, CSS, JavaScript, JSON, and so on
- Validate data based on a JSON schema
- Spin up node and PHP servers
- Live reload browsers when files change

The task runner empowers frontend architects to create a blueprint for the site's creation. Each of the four pillars is wrapped in automation, because it is through automation that we can not only codify our process, but also enforce it. Linting helps to describe and enforce coding standards. Testing suites can be run locally by the developer or inside of continuous integration tools like Jenkins or TravisCI. New builds are compiled and pushed to production consistently with a single click. Documentation is automatically pulled from our code comments, template files, and schemas.

Diving in Deeper

When I first started diving into frontend architecture, before finding Grunt, I became really interested in creating Compass modules. I started off by creating small gems that would let me scaffold new projects, and thinking how I could use a gem to distribute a base set of styles to several websites at a time. While both of these use cases were valid, they express the limit of what I would have been capable of doing without learning a ton more Ruby. And after diving into a few basic Ruby tutorials, I realized that unless I wanted to write Ruby on Rails applications, there weren't many resources for learning to program in Ruby, let alone write Compass modules in Ruby.

After moving to Grunt, one of my greatest wins was that I already knew the language that all of these modules were written in: JavaScript. After working with several modules for a few months, I found that they met 95% of my needs. Now, I'm no Node.js developer, but in several instances I was able to add a feature or fix a bug in a module and push that code upstream. In one case, with the Grunt-PhantomCSS module, I found that I needed to rewrite a majority of the project to fit my workflow. I forked the project, made the necessary changes, and pushed it up to GitHub, where other people found it and started to use it in their own projects. I wasn't just a module user anymore, I was now a module author.

Getting Task Runners into Your Project

My first introduction to Grunt was being tossed into a large, established codebase full of dozens of modules and abstracted code organization—it was anything but easy for a beginner to understand. I eventually learned enough to start modifying the code, and then even add to it, but I'm someone that needs to understand my code from top to bottom before I can really accept and embrace it.

I then started tearing the project down, removing everything I could until I had the most bare-bones, basic setup that still worked. At that point, I understood each line of code in the project and could work my way back up to something more complex. Here is Grunt, at its bare minimum, compiling Sass:

```
module.exports = function(grunt) {
  grunt.loadNpmTasks('grunt-sass');
  grunt.initConfig({
    sass: {
      options: {
      },
      dist: {
        src: 'sass/style.scss',
        dest: 'css/style.css',
      }
    }
  });
  grunt.registerTask('default', [
    'sass'
    ]);
};
```

The preceding code, which simply compiles your *style.scss* to *style.css*, has three distinct code areas:

Loading tasks

Grunt needs to know which of your Node tasks to import into the compile process. If you prefer the idea of just loading all of the packages listed in your *package.json*, the `load-grunt-tasks` (*https://github.com/sindresorhus/load-grunt-tasks*) module will make your life much easier.

Setting configuration

Each task that you load will have a list of configuration options that you can set. In this case, we are just setting the source and destination of the Sass task, but we could also turn on/off sourcemaps, set additional include paths, or change the CSS output style. Each task can also have multiple variations, or targets. You can set up a dev target that has sourcemaps turned on and an expanded output style, then set a dist target that has sourcemaps turned off and the output style set to compressed.

Register custom tasks

In this area, we are able to group various individual tasks into a custom parent task. The default task is what happens when you just type grunt into the command line. You can add more tasks, like Sass Lint, to the default task, or create other custom parent tasks like test or deploy.

Now let's do the same thing in GulpJS:

```
var gulp = require('gulp');
var sass = require('gulp-sass');
gulp.task('default', function () {
    gulp.src('./*.scss')
        .pipe(sass())
        .pipe(gulp.dest('./css'));
});
```

Gulp takes a bit of a different approach than Grunt in defining its tasks. Right off the bat, you can see there is a huge difference in code styles. Grunt is very configuration based, using object notation and defining tasks in one place, then running them in others. Gulp, on the other hand, chains tasks and configuration together and pipes the code from one operation to the next. Let's walk through this code a bit:

Loading tasks

Instead of Grunt's loadNpmTasks function, Gulp uses the traditional Node-based require() syntax. So at the top we load up gulp and gulp-sass, setting them as variables we'll be using shortly.

Creating custom tasks

Again, we see the use of default to indicate what happens when you just type gulp in the command line. But instead of using grunt.registerTask to list the predefined tasks we want to run, we are going to build out the entire process right inside of this function.

The Gulp advantage

The Gulp approach focuses on small, concurrent functions that usually start with collecting a resource, and then passing it through several pipes before sending it to a final destination. There are two major advantages here. First, the concurrent nature of this approach means that processing our Sass isn't blocking our other tasks from running. And second, pipes mean that Gulp can perform multiple operations on a single asset, whereas Grunt would have to write CSS to a temp folder, then perform a second operation on those temp assets.

Is There a Clear Winner?

So which approach is better? Well, that depends on your needs. Grunt is the incumbent in this field, and has the benefit of a larger number of modules. On the other hand, Gulp can be quite a bit faster in larger projects, and the ability to pipe code from one process to another can help keep your project from feeling like one big Rube Goldberg machine.

I've been happily using Grunt for the past few years, though I have been considering taking another look at Gulp and how it would work for my project. But in the end, both of them are great tools, and if there is module support to do the tasks that you need, your decision will probably come down to coding styles.

In the end, a task runner is just a tool. The job of a frontend architect is to create efficient and error-resistant workflows. So if your tooling is helping developers get up and running quickly, giving them a robust environment to quickly develop quality code and then deploy that code to testing, staging, and production environments, you've done your job regardless of your choice in framework.

CHAPTER 10

Red Hat Process

At Red Hat, our frontend development team has the incredible advantage of working multiple sprints ahead of our backend development. We set long-term goals for the features we want to build or update, and once we have a signed-off prototype, we pass it over to our development team to implement.

In past projects, we might have said, "OK, here is the markup we want you to try to output. Please get as close as you can." We would create markup in a siloed set of Mustache or Twig templates, and then ask our development team to create PHP, Ruby, Angular, React, or Ember templates that output the same markup. The problem with this approach is that half of the battle of implementation is trying to get the markup spit out by the backend anywhere close to our prototypes. We'd constantly be tackling bugs that were nothing more than "the markup coming from our CMS does not match our prototype."

Even if we did get the markup to match our prototype, there was always the fear that either the prototype or the CMS code would get out of sync. Changes would be made to one system that were not made in the other, and eventually there was such a crevasse of technical debt that our prototypes couldn't be trusted. We could never be sure that they represented what was actually in production, and any further work on that feature would have to be done directly to the CMS code. The problem was that the CMS and the prototyping tool were not sharing HTML templates, even if they were sharing CSS and JavaScript. In the refactoring of the Red Hat theme, we had an opportunity to tackle this "last mile" issue once and for all.

Conquering the Last Mile

Our problem was that Drupal had a very opinionated rendering engine, and it was very difficult to prototype the markup that Drupal would render without actually running Drupal itself. So we decided to upend the Drupal rendering pipeline and insert our own solution. We wanted a solution that could be shared between our prototyping tool, Drupal, WordPress, or any other platform that wanted to use our design system. We started with the Twig templating language, as it was mature and robust, and had both PHP and Node compiling engines.

Now that we had a universal rendering engine that allowed us to use the same template files in our prototyping tool as we did in production, we never again had to worry about translating our templates from one system to another. Once we created a pattern in our style guide, we could document the data set required to produce that design, and pass that off to our backend developers to implement. In a way, we had created a design system API, or a theme as a service, where our users had a simple, defined interface that accepted data input and returned identical HTML regardless of the platform.

A Standard Set of Deliverables

This relationship between data and template quickly turned into a very important part of our design system. Our developers started asking to have a list of template variables, the variable content types, and which of them were required. These were important requests, and we wanted to provide our developers with the most complete information possible. This all led to the standard set of deliverable files that we now ship with all of our components and layouts.

The standard set of component deliverable files is:

JSON schema
> The schema defines the various attributes (variables) of the component, their content types, and which of them are required.

Template file
> This Twig file accepts a set of data defined by the JSON schema. Optional data is gated behind `if` statements, and data arrays are looped through.

Sass partial

All of the component styles originate from this single Sass partial. It gets compiled into the primary *style.css* file, or can be loaded in as an individual CSS file.

Visual regression tests

This file describes all of the browser widths and component states that will be tested each time our visual regression tests are run. These tests must pass before any new code is merged into the design system.

Testing data

This file allows us to create test-specific data to get complete test coverage and test edge cases.

Documentation

The documentation file is a Markdown file that will be fed into our documentation tool, Hologram (*https://github.com/trulia/holo gram*). It provides a description and list of capabilities for the component. The documentation page also provides a visual representation of the component and includes a live editor that allows us to test various content and create direct links to share that content combination with others.

Documentation data

The documentation data is the starting data that will be ingested by the documentation page to create the initial view.

All of these files are valuable deliverables for feature creation, but one of them serves as the cornerstone of this entire process, and is often the first file to be created: the JSON schema. No other file in this set of deliverables offers a better description of the needs and capabilities of this feature as the JSON schema. Whenever there is a change made to the functionality of a component, that change originates in the schema and is then spread out to the other files within the component. It is because of the importance of this single file that we call this process a *schema-driven design system*.

Schema-Driven Design System

By now, *test-driven design* is a pretty common and accepted practice in software development. Before writing a line of code, we write a suite of tests that describe what the code is supposed to accomplish.

Then, when we start our feature we have failing tests, but as we write our code we eventually get all of the tests passing.

The idea of a *schema-driven design system* is very similar, but instead of tests written in NodeUnit or PHPUnit that describe the proper functionality of an application, we create schemas in JSON. These files describe the correct data structure for a component in our design system. In employing a schema-driven design system, we focus first on content and the user's interface with our design, instead of the markup and CSS. Let's look at a simplified version of a schema we might use on the Red Hat website and see how this information helps us make better decisions for our design system.

The following JSON schema describes a display that contains a headline and two or three logo images:

```
{
  "type": "object",
  "properties": {
    "headline": {
      "type": "string",
      "format": "text"
    },
    "body": {
      "type": "object",
      "oneOf": [
        {
          "title": "Two Up",
          "required": ["logos", "layout"],
          "properties": {
            "layout": {
              "type": "string",
              "enum": ["2up"],
              "options": {
                "hidden": true
              }
            },
            "logos": {
              "type": "array",
              "format": "tabs",
              "minItems": 2,
              "maxItems": 2,
              "items": {
                "$ref": "#/definitions/logo"
              }
            }
          }
        },
        {
```

```
            "title": "Three Up",
            "properties": {
              "layout": {
                "type": "string",
                "enum": ["3up"],
                "options": {
                  "hidden": true
                }
              },
              "logos": {
                "format": "tabs",
                "type": "array",
                "minItems": 3,
                "maxItems": 3,
                "items": {
                  "$ref": "#/definitions/logo"
                }
              }
            },
            "required": ["logos", "layout"]
          }
        ]
      }
    },
    "required": ["body"],
    "definitions": {
      "logo": {
        "title": "Logo",
        "type": "object",
        "oneOf": [
          {
            "title": "Upload File",
            "properties": {
              "file": {
                "title": "Logo File",
                "description": "Upload your logo",
                "type": "string",
                "format": "file"
              }
            },
            "required": ["file"]
          },
          {
            "title": "Paste URL",
            "properties": {
              "url": {
                "title": "Logo URL",
                "description": "Paste a URL to your logo",
                "type": "string",
                "format": "url"
              }
```

```
          },
          "required": ["url"]
        }
      ]
    }
  }
}
```

At 91 lines long, this might seem quite verbose for such a simple component, but let's walk through each section and discuss how each piece helps to drive not just the data structure, but the editor UI and the outputted HTML.

Line 2:

```
"type": "object",
"required": ["body"],
"properties" {
    "headline": {
      ...
```

Every schema we create is a description of the data that needs to be collected and eventually passed on to a template or view. Each property of a schema represents either a single piece of data, or a group of data that will be described in a subschema. So after stating that this schema will describe an object of key/value pairs, we state that only the body field is required.

Line 5:

```
"headline": {
 "type": "string",
 "format": "text"
},
```

Our first property, the headline, is optional since it is not listed in the required array above. We know that it is a string, which tells us how this value will be stored in a database.

We also know that the format is simply text, which describes the form element used to gather the headline. The format could also be textarea, url, color, range, or any other valid HTML5 input types. In the end, the value saved is still a string, but we are able to hint to the editor how to display the input.

Line 9:

```
"body": {
 "type": "object",
```

The body, our second property, is of the type `object` and therefore it's not just a single value, but a group of values, which have their own schema. In this case, though, there are two possible schemas that could be used here. Let me explain why.

For this logo design, we were asked to create a layout that could accept either two or three logos. Figure 10-1 shows the mockup we were given.

Figure 10-1. The "three up" mockup

Anyone who's seen this design before will quickly realize that there is an important piece of information missing. What happens to the layout when there are only two logos? Does the layout remain the same, with simply a blank space where the logo was? Or do we switch to a different layout, giving each logo more space? These two options are illustrated in Figures 10-2 and 10-3, respectively.

Figure 10-2. Same layout, one less element

Figure 10-3. Use up all available space

The power of our schemas is that we don't have to leave this question up in the air. We can define what happens when we have two logos, or when we have three. The way we do that is by defining the two different schemas that are possible, one with two logos, and the other with three. We'll do that starting on line 11, where we define the options for our body schema:

Line 11:

```
"oneOf": [
  {
    ...
  },
  {
    ...
  }
]
```

JSON schema has a few keywords that allow us to be a bit more flexible with our schemas. They include `oneOf`, `anyOf`, and `allOf`. We'll be using `oneOf` here, which means that our data needs to conform to "one of" the following schemas, not "all of" them or "any of" them.

As you can see, `oneOf` takes an array of objects. Our body data needs to validate against one, and only one, of the contained schemas.

Line 13:

```
"title": "Two Up",
"required": ["logos", "layout"],
"properties": {
  "layout": {
    "type": "string",
    "enum": ["2up"],
    "options": {
      "hidden": true
    }
  },
  "logos": {...}
```

The first schema is a "two up" schema. It has a title of `Two Up`, which we can use in the UI when switching from one schema to the other. The `required` field simply tells this subschema which of the listed properties are required to satisfy the schema. Here we're stating that both are required.

The first property `layout` is unique in that it is not something we expect the user to set, but it is a value that still needs to be stored and passed to our template. Because this value is required, the only way to satisfy the schema is to pass the string 2up as the layout value.

If the specifications required us to allow the user to choose which layout they wanted to use, we could update this enum value to ["2up", "3up"] instead. Because we've decided to not let the user select the layout, we added a "hidden": true to our property options. This is a cue to hide this value from the UI, but still pass a value to our template.

Now that the layout for this schema is set, we turn to the logos that we'd like our user to upload.

Line 23:

```
"logos": {
  "type": "array",
  "minItems": 2,
  "maxItems": 2,
  "format": "tabs",
  "items": {
    "$ref": "#/definitions/logo"
  }
}
```

The logos property is another unique property in that the data it'll be storing is neither a string nor an object, but an array. Because it's an array, there are several things we need to know about it. For instance, we need to determine the minimum and maximum items in the array, how we should format this data in our UI, and the schema for each of the items in that array.

For our logos, we set minItems and maxItems to 2. This means that the only option we have is to pass in two items, which is great because our layout is expecting two.

In the same way that we hinted that our headline property should be displayed as a text input, here we've specified that the format should be a tabbed layout. Now, "tabbed" layout means nothing to the JSON schema. These are merely hints that we can pass on to the UI ingesting our schemas. It is up to each implementation to determine what "tabs" mean, so if the format is completely ignored, the schema and data produced are no less valid.

Lastly, we define our items, which is a keyword that allows us to define what schema our array items will adhere to. In this instance, $ref signifies that we're using a JSON pointer. This allows us to point to an external definition rather than define one here. The value #/definitions/logo instructs the pointer to look at the local schema root #, and then return the object at definitions/logo, which we can find down on line 60.

The reason that we use a reference here is that both our "two up" schema and our "three up" schema use the exact same definition for a logo. This means that we can create our two schemas, and only specify the values that change.

We aren't limited to internal references either, as the $ref value can reference other schema files too. This allows you to create commonly used schemas in separate files and access them from other schemas. In this case, we opted to use a local reference, so let's jump down and see what this reference is referring to.

Line 60:

```
"logo": {
  "title": "Logo",
  "type": "object",
  "oneOf": [...]
```

Here, we start to define the logo object. Again, we give our object a more human-readable title, even if it is just capitalization, and then we state that the rest of this object conforms to oneOf the following schemas. You see, we want to allow for two different methods for inputting our logos, and they each require their own schema values.

The first is in case the user wants to upload a file, and the second is if the user opts to paste in a URL.

line 64:

```
{
  "title": "Upload File",
    "properties": {
      "file": {
        "title": "Logo File",
        "description": "Upload your logo",
        "type": "string",
        "format": "file"
    }
  },
  "required": ["file"]
},
{
  "title": "Paste URL",
  "properties": {
```

```
    "url": {
     "title": "Logo URL",
     "description": "Paste a URL to your logo",
     "type": "string",
     "format": "url"
    }
   },
   "required": ["url"]
  }
```

At this point, we get a chance to set the title of this oneOf selection, as well as the title of the property we'll call file. The important value here is the format value of file, which will tell our UI to provide a "choose file" dialog box. But if the user would prefer to paste in a URL, then they can switch to the second schema, which provides a URL field, including the necessary help text.

Moving to the Twig File

The last step of this process is to move all this information into the template file. Let's first take a look at what some valid data will look like:

```
{
  "headline": "This is my headline",
  "body": {
    "layout": "2up",
    "logos": [
      {
        "url": "http://www.fea.pub/my-logo.png"
      },
      {
        "file": "path/to/my-other-logo.png"
      }
    ]
  }
}
```

This is what our Twig template might look like:

```
<div class="logo-wall">
  {% if headline %}
    <h1 class="logo-wall-headline">{{headline}}</h1>
  {% endif %}
  <div class="logo-wall-logos" data-layout="{{body.layout}}">
    {% for logo in body.logos %}
      <img class="logo-wall-logo"
        src="{{ logo.file ?: logo.url }}" />
    {% endfor %}
```

```
    </div>
  </div>
```

The first thing we are able to glean from the schema is about the headline. Not only do we know the key for that value, headline, but we also know that the value is not required. So we first create a test in Twig to see if headline is set, and if it is, we print it inside of an H1 tag.

Moving into the body of our schema, we use the layout value to set our data-layout attribute. We'll handle what this actually does within our CSS, but for now we can be confident that if the data source has three images, this body.layout will equal 3up, and if there are only two, it'll be 2up.

Lastly, we know that logos is an array of objects with either a URL or a file string. Twig gives us a simple method to check if logo.file exists, and then use that value if it does exist, or use logo.url if it does not exist.

So in the end, this single schema provides us with the following:

- A definition of the content model with all possible fields, their data type, prefered input type, and which of them are required.
- A method for validating the data before it's passed along to the template.
- A set of definitions needed to create a template file that accounts for every possible variation in the data.
- A description of the UI we'd prefer our users encounter when entering this data. Figure 10-4 shows an example of our schema rendered with the JSON-editor library (*http://bit.ly/1FKio8h*).

This is a powerful combination of benefits to be gained from 91 lines of JSON. For the design system that we are creating, it is the perfect vehicle for communicating concepts and ideas that would otherwise take paragraphs of text to convey properly.

Figure 10-4. Jeremy Dorn's JSON editor

Every day that I work within this system I am amazed at how well these schemas allow us to convey changes or additions to a template and the methods that developers should use to interface with them. These schemas have removed a majority of the guesswork that accompanied previous asset handoffs.

By following a public standard, we are constantly finding third-party tools that add value and functionality to our design system. Our strict adherence to a schema system has paid off in so many areas that I am confident I will never create another design system without them again. This is a schema-driven design system.

PART IV

The Testing Pillar

As frontend architects, one of our greatest roles is to oversee the development of the website and design system, but anyone who has been in a project of significant scope knows that it is impossible for a single person to oversee every aspect of a project. With team members numbering in the dozens, weekly commits in the hundreds, and lines of code in the thousands, it is beyond reason to think that a single person can evaluate the impact of every single piece of code entering the system. Yet this level of evaluation is exactly what we need to be doing.

New code can introduce bugs or regressions in many different ways. Some regressions will affect the outcome of system computation, resulting in incorrect product prices, while others affect the ability of a user to successfully check out using the site shopping cart. Other regressions are visual, and while the user can still technically complete the task, the experience is made difficult because of a broken or inconsistent user interface. Lastly, even if the user interface is complete and the shopping cart functionality is working properly, the performance of the site might still render the checkout process virtually impossible on given devices or from certain geographic regions. These different types of regression stem from very different parts of your codebase, but they all have a similar impact: loss of sales. Fortunately, each of them has a very similar solution: testing!

While we as architects cannot spend all of our time watching every single line of code being committed, we are able to set up various suites of tests to verify our application is working properly.

Here are a few things to remember when you start looking at planning test coverage for your application:

- Tests are written while the site is being built, or even before actual code is written.
- They are living code, committed with or next to the system repository.
- All tests must pass before any code is merged into the master branch.
- Running the suite on the master branch should always return a passing response.

This means that no code should ever be merged that breaks the system's ability to calculate values, perform critical business actions, display the correct UI, or deliver a performant experience. So instead of trying to oversee thousands of lines of code, an architect should focus on creating a system for quality and complete test coverage.

CHAPTER 11
Unit Testing

Unit testing is the process of breaking down your application to the smallest possible functions, and creating a repeatable, automated test that should continually produce the same result. These tests are the heart and soul of your application. They provide the foundation that all future code is built upon. Without unit tests, it is possible that a seldom-used function could remain broken for months without anyone noticing. With unit tests, every system function can be verified before a single line of code is even merged into the master branch, let alone pushed to production.

As a frontend architect, your primary role is making sure that developers have the tools necessary to be as efficient as possible. Unit tests are one of those essential tools for building an application of any scale. Whether your application logic is written mostly in a backend or frontend language, there are plenty of options to fit your workflow. No matter if you are running PHPUnit with PHP, NodeUnit with Node, or QUnit with JavaScript, you will find mature, stable platforms to build your tests upon.

Though your technology stack (and the tests associated with it) might be left up to the software architect, it is quite probable that your frontend developers will also be writing code that requires tests. Therefore it is important to become familiar with as many of the suites as possible. Acquiring mastery, or even proficiency, with all of them is not something we typically have the luxury of doing, but a solid understanding of the basic concepts will help you and your team write more testable code, and get up to speed with any framework quickly.

Let's review some of these basic concepts now, and then we'll have an opportunity to look at the code in action.

The Unit

"Do one thing, and do it well" is the mantra when you are building an application with unit tests. Too often we write functions that try to do too many things. Not only is this very inefficient, as it does not lead to reuse, but it also makes these functions very difficult to test.

Consider this simple function: given a customer's address, the function determines the cost to ship a product to that customer from the nearest distribution center.

Let's break this function down a bit. The first thing that happens is that our function uses the address to find the nearest distribution center. Using that distribution center address, the function then determines the distance between the center and the customer's address. Lastly, using that distance, the function calculates the shipping cost to move the package from point A to point B. So even though we have a single function, the function is performing three separate actions:

1. Look up distribution center nearest to given address.
2. Calculate a distance between two addresses.
3. Evaluate shipping cost for a given distance.

Going back to the idea of "doing one thing, and doing it well," it is pretty obvious that we could better accomplish our address lookup action by combining three separate functions. When our action is split up, we get a function that allows us to find the nearest distribution center to any given address, a function that calculates the distance between two given addresses, and a function that returns the cost of shipping a product any given distance.

More Reuse

Now these three functions can be used throughout our entire application, not just for calculating shipping costs. If we have another part of the application that needs to find a distribution center, or to calculate the distance between two addresses, those functions have already been created. We aren't reproducing small units of functionality over and over again in separate, larger functions.

Better Testing

Instead of testing every possible way our application might determine shipping, we can instead test each individual, reusable function. As our application grows, the number of new functions needed to create new features decreases. In the end, we have a smaller number of less complex functions performing more advanced functionality.

Test-Driven Development

When most of us first approached unit testing, we probably wrote up some functionality that met a business goal (such as our shipping example) and then worked to refactor it into smaller, reusable, testable bits. At that point, we would consider the tests we'd want to write. Test-driven development (TDD) turns that idea upside down by putting the tests first, before any functional code is even written.

But if we write tests for functions we haven't created, won't they all fail? Exactly! TDD sets out to describe how a system should work when written properly, and creates a path for us to create that system.

For our shipping example, TDD would write three tests, one for each of the three functions required to perform this business function. The developer's job is to turn those failing tests into passing tests. First, we write a function that properly looks up the location of the nearest distribution center, and we have one passing test. We then move on to measuring distance and calculating shipping, and finish with three functions that make their associate test pass.

With this done, not only have we built the functionality required for our application to look up shipping cost, but we have complete test coverage for these functions.

A Test-Driven Example

At its core, unit testing is extremely simple. The basic idea is to call the function being tested, passing it preset values and describing what the result should be. Let's look at how we'd do this for our function that calculates the shipping cost for a given distance:

```javascript
function calculateShipping(distance) {
  switch (distance) {
    case (distance < 25):
      shipping = 4;
      break;
    case (distance < 100):
      shipping = 5;
      break;
    case (distance < 1000):
      shipping = 6;
      break;
    case (distance >= 1000):
      shipping = 7;
      break;
  }
  return shipping;
}

QUnit.test('Calculate Shipping', function(assert) {
  assert.equal(calculateShipping(24), 4, "24 Miles");
  assert.equal(calculateShipping(99), 5, "99 Miles");
  assert.equal(calculateShipping(999), 6, "999 Miles");
  assert.equal(calculateShipping(1000), 7, "1000 Miles");
};
```

QUnit (*https://qunitjs.com/*) has several operators for testing assertions, including ok() for testing Boolean values or deepEqual() for comparing complex objects. In this case, we are using the equal() function to compare the value returned by calculateShipping() with the expected result. As long as calculateShipping(24) returns a value of 4 (which it will here), our test will pass. The third value, 24 Miles, is used to label the pass/fail statement in the test output.

With these tests (and others) in place, we have a single suite to run that will assert whether or not our system is working. If someone were to change the name of the calculateShipping() function or modify the shipping prices, this test would return failures, and we could fix the problem before offending code was pushed to production.

QUnit is capable of doing much more than the preceding example. For instance, it is capable of performing tests on both synchronous and asynchronous functions. QUnit can also interact with the web page that the tests are loaded on (remember, this is all just Java-

Script). So if your tests include values being returned when a mouse is clicked or a key is pressed, QUnit has you covered there too.

How Much Coverage Is Enough?

Determining proper test coverage can be a very difficult balancing act. If you aren't running test-driven development (where nothing is written without tests), it will be important to determine how much coverage is enough coverage. Test everything, and your development process can get bogged down. Don't test enough, and you risk regressions slipping through.

Fixing the Gaps

If you are implementing unit tests on an existing project, you most likely won't have the time or budget to write 100% test coverage for current functionality. And that's OK! The beauty of test coverage is that even a single test adds value to a system. So when determining where to start writing tests, look for the biggest wins first. Sometimes the biggest win is writing tests for the simplest parts of your system. Just like paying off your small credit card debt before trying to tackle your larger debt, writing some simple, but still valuable, tests will be a great place to build momentum.

Once you have a working suite providing some basic coverage, start looking at the parts of the system that are either the most critical, or have had recurring trouble in the past. Create stories for your backlog for each of them and make sure to pull them forward as often as possible.

Coverage from the Start

If you are fortunate enough to be starting a new project as a frontend architect, your job is not just to get a testing framework set up, but to make sure that the development process itself is prepared for unit testing. Just like writing documentation or performing code review, writing unit tests take time! You'll need to make sure that any story requiring tests is given the extra time required to write and verify the necessary test coverage.

At Red Hat, every user story starts with a set of tasks and time to develop and verify the test coverage required for that feature. If a new feature is estimated to take eight hours of development time to complete, we make sure to schedule another two hours to write and verify test coverage. This additional time can often be a hard sell, so the frontend architect frequently needs to play diplomat and salesperson. Even though this is a 25% increase in the time, we know that this test coverage will save us dozens of hours in the future that would have been spent tracking down bugs.

As I said earlier, not every feature requires the same amount of test coverage. But the assumption is that every story *starts* with tasks for test coverage. As long as those tasks are only removed when everyone agrees that coverage isn't necessary, we can be confident that any feature requiring coverage is given the time needed to finish that task.

CHAPTER 12

Performance Testing

The purpose of any testing is to protect users from a degraded or broken experience, and poor website performance is one of the quickest ways to give your users a degraded and broken experience. Therefore, performance testing, while not a test that points out system or visual regressions, is an important part of our testing arsenal.

Performance testing measures key metrics that affect a user's ability to use your website, including page weight, number of requests, time to first byte (TTFB), load time, and scrolling performance.

The key to performance testing is to set a proper budget and stick to it. How you set the budget and stick to it will determine how effective the tests will be in your project.

Setting a Performance Budget

Creating a performance budget means setting target values for each key metric and then continually testing those metrics before each code merge or deployment. If any of the tests fail, the new feature will need to be adjusted, or some other feature may need to be removed.

As with financial budgets, very few people are really excited about the prospect of performance budgets. To most, a budget means spending less, getting less, having less fun, and most importantly...less! Less isn't much fun in a world where we are always being told that we deserve more. As designers, we feel that our creativity is being stifled if we can't toss around hi-res images and full-screen video with reckless abandon. As developers, we think that we can't do our job without a CSS framework, a couple Java-Script frameworks, and dozens of jQuery plug-ins. Less is no fun!

As a person that has been living within a financial budget for the past four years, I certainly understand what it means to not get everything I want. On the other hand, when I do make a large, budgeted purchase, I do so without a single bit of guilt or debt. In the same way, performance budgets allow us to "spend" our budget responsibly, and without regret.

Just like fiscal discipline and financial budgets, UX discipline and a performance budget can help us to achieve our ultimate goals, which include a performant website and an engaged user.

While a financial budget is typically based off one's income, a per-formance budget has more to do with external factors than internal ones.

Competitive Baseline

One method of determining your performance budget is to look at your competition. While saying "at least I'm better than so-and-so" is no excuse for a poorly performing website, it does ensure that you have a competitive advantage.

Start by looking at a few of your key competitors' homepages and other key landing pages, and then compare load times, page weight, and other key metrics with your own website. The goal here isn't to just match their metrics. You want to make sure you are beating them by 20% or more. So if your competitor's product listing page loads in 3 seconds, make sure that your site loads its product listing page in 2.4 seconds or less. This 20% advantage over your competi-tor is the difference required for a user to recognize the difference between the two tasks.

This is not something you do just once, but something that needs to be monitored regularly. You can be assured that your competitors are looking for ways to improve and optimize their own sites. And if they had been looking at your site to determine their budgets, you've now pushed them to reduce their budgets as well!

Averaged Baseline

Regardless of your competition, it is always important to compare your performance baselines to industry averages and general best practices. There is no reason to settle for mediocre just because your competition is throwing off the curve.

HTTPArchive (*http://httparchive.org/*) is a great service that measures and records the average value of various website metrics across almost half a million websites. As of April 2015, here are a few values of note:

- Page weight: 2,061 KB
- Total requests: 99
- Cacheable resources: 46%

Therefore, if you want your website to feel faster than most websites, you might consider setting a goal of having a 1,648 KB website, that is served with 79 requests, of which 44 are cacheable. This will put you 20% ahead of the average website.

So now that we know a few methods for setting our budget, what are the budget items we need to consider when setting our tests up?

Raw Metrics

The most basic test of website performance is to look at the assets that are required to render it. How heavy are those assets, and how many of them are there?

Page Weight

Websites are getting fatter! Between April 2014 and April of 2015, the average website grew from 1,762 to 2,061 kilobytes, a 17% increase year over year. Reaching back to April of 2011, the average page was a skimpy 769 KB!

While page weight is not the only factor affecting the load time of your website, it certainly plays a large part. Page weight also has another side effect as we remember that more and more people are accessing our sites on mobile devices, and they are paying to download those bytes. The heavier your page, the more you are going to be costing your customers, especially in developing nations. Consider checking out What Does My Site Cost? (*http://whatdoesmysite*

cost.com/) to see what that new carousel is costing your mobile customers in Germany.

When looking to reduce the weight of your pages, there are a few obvious places to start:

- Images make up 61% of an average website's page weight.
  - Optimize your PNG files. Consider reducing the quality of some JPEG files.
  - Take advantage of the new responsive image `<picture>` tag and `srcset` attribute to download appropriately sized images.
  - Set a budget and don't add image weight without removing another image.
- Too many custom fonts will quickly weigh your page down.
  - Set a font budget and consider not adding that second or third font.
  - Consider necessary font weights, as each font weight adds kilobyte weight to the font file.
  - While icon fonts are great, be mindful of the file size, as they can grow large quite quickly. Split the font up if one set is used for one section of the website, and another set for others. Also consider using inline SVGs instead, as you'll gain many of the benefits of icon fonts while only needing to load the required SVGs.
- JS frameworks, jQuery plug-ins, and CSS frameworks often add a great deal of weight for little reward.
  - Many sites are moving away from jQuery, as vanilla JS is sufficient for their needs, especially if targeting modern browsers.
  - jQuery plug-ins, while they might offer some "wiz-bang" functionality, can often add significant weight to your site. Consider if the same thing could be done with CSS for modern browsers with reasonable fallbacks for older ones.
  - Large JS frameworks like Angular or Ember might accomplish what you need done, but might come with more weight than required to get the job done. If all you need from Angular is the view layer, you might be better off using React or even Mustache.
  - CSS frameworks are often a kitchen sink. They include every little imaginable style you could ever possibly need. While this might be great for prototyping, starting your

website with hundreds of kilobytes of CSS and JS is putting yourself in quite a hole before you even write a line of code.

- Take advantage of minification and compression.
  - JavaScript can be programmatically minified during your build process, and your servers can be set up to gzip files before sending them to the browser. These are both vital steps to reducing page weight.

Number of HTTP Requests

The browser is required to perform an HTTP request for every single file needed to fully render a page. Because each browser has a limited number of concurrent HTTP requests it can make, a large number of individual files means that the browser has to make numerous round trips to the server. The effect of these rounds trips is compounded on slower networks, so limiting the number of round trips needed to gather the required files will pay off greatly.

You can reduce the number of round trips in a few ways:

- Reduce the number of HTTP requests.
  - Instead of serving up dozens of individual CSS and JavaScript files, concatenate them into single files.
  - Combine individual image files into a single image map or icon font. You'll find many great tools to do this for you automatically (Compass, Grunt/Gulp plug-ins).
  - Lazy-load assets not required for initial page load. This could be JavaScript that isn't needed until the user interacts with the page, or images that are far below the initial load window.
- Increase the number of assets retrieved per round trip.
  - Splitting up your assets across different servers (or CDNs) will allow the browser to pull down more assets per round trip, as the limitations on concurrent connections is per server.

Timing Metrics

Regardless of the number and size of your site's assets, there are a number of other timing metrics that impact a user's perceptions of your site's performance.

Time to first byte (TTFB)
Time to first byte is the number of milliseconds between the browser requesting the web page, and the first byte being received by the browser. It is a measurement of the paths between the browser and the server, including DNS lookup, initial connection, and data receipt. This value is not the best judge of a website's performance, but it is a valuable number to keep an eye on.

Time to start render
A more useful time measurement is the "time to start render." This measurement is the time at which the user starts to see content on the page. This means that any blocking files have been loaded and the browser is able to start drawing out the DOM. You can improve this number by deferring blocking JS/CSS, putting critical CSS inline in the page head, replacing image assets with data URIs, and lazy-loading any blocking content that it loads after the document has completely rendered.

Time to document complete
Once all of the initially requested assets have been loaded, the document is considered to be "complete." Time to document complete doesn't include assets pulled in by JavaScript, so lazy-loading assets won't increase this metric.

Hybrid Metrics

Hybrid metrics don't measure a discrete value; they are scores based on numbers performance indicators.

PageSpeed Score

PageSpeed (*http://bit.ly/pagespeed_insights*) is a website tool and Chrome extension made by Google that analyzes the performance and usability of a website, providing a score out of 100 and explaining ways that the user can improve that score. Tests include:

- Presence of render-blocking JavaScript or CSS
- Landing page redirects
- Image optimization
- File minification
- Server response time
- Server compression
- Browser caching
- Tap target size

- Viewport properly configured
- Legible font sizes

Speed Index

As stated on the project page, the speed index (*http://bit.ly/spd-index*) is the average time at which visible parts of the page are displayed. It is expressed in milliseconds and dependent on size of the view port.

This hybrid timing metric provides a score that takes into account many of the metrics just discussed, and combines them with a measurement of what the user is actually able to see of your site as it loads. Speed index is one of the best measurements of actual end-user experience.

Setting Up Performance Tests

Now that we know what types of metrics we can test and how to set performance budgets, let's take a quick look at a few methods for automating the testing process. Whether you are testing a single website or dozens of them, no one wants to perform these measurements manually.

Grunt PageSpeed

The first tool we'll look at for automating this workflow is Grunt PageSpeed (*https://www.npmjs.com/package/grunt-pagespeed*). As the name implies, this is a Grunt plug-in that allows us to run Google's PageSpeed test on our website. So rather than plugging your URL into the test page or using a Chrome extension, you can run this Grunt task before every merge request or continuous integration build.

To set up Grunt PageSpeed, start with the standard commands to install and require our plug-in:

```
$ npm install grunt-pagespeed --save-dev

// Added to Gruntfile.js
grunt.loadNpmTasks('grunt-pagespeed');

// Added to grunt.initConfig inside of Gruntfile.js
  pagespeed: {
    options: {
```

```
    nokey: true,
    url: "http://redhat.com"
  },
  desktop: {
    options: {
      paths: ["/en", "/en/services"],
      locale: "en_US",
      strategy: "desktop",
      threshold: 80
    }
  },
  mobile: {
    options: {
      paths: ["/en", "/en/services"],
      locale: "en_US",
      strategy: "mobile",
      threshold: 80
    }
  }
}
```

This code will allow us to automatically run both desktop and mobile tests on an array of pages inside of our base URL (in this case, *http://www.redhat.com/*). As long as our score comes back over 80, the tests will pass. If it is below 80, we'll get a failing test, which signifies that changes need to be made to hit our threshold again.

Grunt Perfbudget

Another great Grunt tool is Grunt Perfbudget (*https://github.com/ tkadlec/grunt-perfbudget*). This Grunt plug-in taps into Marcel Duran's WebPageTest API (*https://github.com/marcelduran/ webpagetest-api*), allowing us to programmatically pull results from WebPageTest (*http://www.webpagetest.org/*) and compare them with our set budgets. If you haven't used WebPageTest yet, you'll be in for a treat. It is able to test numerous metrics for your site while simulating different types of connections and locations around the globe. I won't get into everything the site can do, but after five minutes of viewing the results for your own site, I'm confident you'll love the wide array of information it provides.

So let's see what this looks like set up in Grunt:

You can currently get a limited-use API key at the WebPageTest website (*http://www.webpaget est.org/getkey.php*).

```
$ npm install grunt-perfbudget --save-dev

// Added to Gruntfile.js
grunt.loadNpmTasks('grunt-perfbudget');

perfbudget: {
  default: {
    options: {
      url: 'http://www.redhat.com/en',
      key: 'SEE_NOTE_ABOVE',
      budget: {
        visualComplete: '4000',
        SpeedIndex: '1500'
      }
    }
  }
}
```

This setup allows us to automatically run the Red Hat homepage through the entire WebPageTest suite of tests, and check the returned values against the budgets I have set. In this case, I have set my Visually Complete timing metric to 4,000 milliseconds and the Speed Index to 1,500. If either of those tests comes back above our budget, we get a big error message telling us to revisit the most recent code push and see what we did to break our budget.

Conclusion

With some proper automated testing, and a competitive budget in place, you'll be in a good position to continue developing features and making improvements to your website while being sure that none of the changes you push out ever break your budget.

CHAPTER 13

Visual Regression Testing

Tell me if this is a familiar scene: you've been working on your website contact form for the last few weeks, trying to tweak and nudge the form fields until they look exactly like the Photoshop mockup. You've meticulously compared every margin, padding, border, and line height. Your lead generation tool is now "pixel perfect," and the product owner agrees: "This is the contact form to end all contact forms." With this code securely committed, you move on to your next task and stop having recurring nightmares about browser drop-down rendering discrepancies.

Weeks later, you are surprised to find a familiar sight in your ticket queue: the contact form. Some designer, business analyst, or quality assurance engineer took a ruler to your design and compared it to the latest Photoshop comp, and found a list of discrepancies.

But why?! How?! Did someone break your code? Did someone change the design? Tracking down the culprit is a luxury you do not have time to pursue. So you sit down with a list of tweaks and get to work hoping that this is the last time you'll have to touch this contact form, but resign yourself to the fact that you'll probably see it a few more times before the site launches.

The Usual Suspects

My favorite sound in the world is the cry of a decision maker as they scream how "feature X is totally broken!" Translated into developer terms, this usually means that a few of the font styles are incorrect, or that some vertical rhythm needs fixing. It doesn't matter if the feature had been signed off and agreed upon, there is a difference between what is live and the specific version of the Photoshop file the decision maker has been poring over for the past week.

Having had this happen to me over and over again, let me explore a few of the common reasons that this merry-go-round has so much trouble stopping and letting you off.

Unknowing Developers

Any code that you can write without defect can be broken by just a few errant lines from another developer. Someone else, working on some other form component, didn't realize that the classes they were styling were shared with your contact form. These changes could have happened in the weeks since your code was committed, or they could have been written at the exact same time as you were working.

Small cosmetic changes to unrelated pages are often overlooked by the QA team. With dozens or even hundreds of pages to test, there is no way that they would catch a two-pixel change to a label's font size.

Inconsistent Designs

Allow me to let you in on a dirty little secret about Photoshop. When a designer changes the font size of a form label in one file, it doesn't magically change in all of the designer's PSD files. Sadly, there isn't a single *sheet* prescribing all of the element *styles* in a *cascading* fashion. Even if all of the designers communicate this font size change, this doesn't magically update every PSD trapped in an email thread, Basecamp conversation, or Dropbox folder.

Depending on which designer, business analyst, or QA engineer is reviewing the contact form, and which version of whatever PSD they happen to be looking at, there is a 9 in 10 chance on any given day that your form has a defect (and therefore is totally broken). A new story is created to address these defects, and you can only hope that the changes you are making aren't going to make even more work for you the next time a designer takes a peek at the contact form.

Waffling Decision Makers

According to the law of infinite probability, given enough features, pored over by enough decision makers, there is a 100% chance that someone will find something that they want to change.

Change is inevitable, and given the proper development model, it is completely acceptable. But when change masquerades as defects (or a distinction is never made), developers end up spending a ton of time building features that are nothing more than prototypes.

There is nothing wrong with prototyping a feature before releasing it to the public—in fact, it's generally a really good practice! But prototypes need to consist of quickly iterated designs ending in a final, agreed-upon product. Asking a developer to create a single prototype every sprint cycle, and then revising it every other sprint, is not only a great way to hobble a developer's productivity, but is a horribly inefficient way to prototype.

A Tested Solution

While each of these scenarios highlights some deeper, organizational issues, they can all be mitigated by a single thing: proper test coverage. For this type of coverage, we aren't testing the valid response of a JavaScript function, but rather we're capturing the visual appearance of an approved design system and validating that we have not deviated from that system. Capturing these visual regressions before they are committed is the key to maintaining a sustainable design system.

Visual regression testing allows us to make visual comparisons between the correct (baseline) versions of our site and versions in development or just about to be deployed (new). The process is nothing more than taking a picture of the baseline and comparing it to the new, looking for differences in the pixels.

With these baseline images either committed to the repo, or marked approved in some testing database, we now have a record of the exact signed-off, agreed-upon pixels that make up any particular feature (in our case, a contact form). Before any line of code is committed back to the master branch, visual regression testing gives us a method to test every feature in our site, and make sure that nothing unexpected has visibly changed.

We will also be guarded against bug reports that are nothing more than inconsistencies from one PSD to another. With a signed-off baseline committed to our codebase, we can run our tests and confidently reply that our code is correct, and that the error must be in the Photoshop file. In the same way, we will be able to discern between actual bugs and YACR (yet another change request).

The Many Faces of Visual Regression Testing

Visual regression testing comes in many different flavors, using a variety of technologies and workflows. While there are new tools being released into the open source community all the time, they typically include a combination of a small set of features. Here are a few of the categories that most tools fall into:

Page-based diffing
Wraith (*https://github.com/BBC-News/wraith*) is a good example of page-based diffing. It has a simple YAML setup file that makes it very easy to compare a large list of pages between two different sources. This approach is best used when you aren't expecting any differences between the two sources, such as when you are comparing pages from your live site with the same pages in staging, just about to be deployed.

Component-based diffing
BackstopJS (*https://github.com/garris/BackstopJS*) is a great tool for doing component- or selector-based diffing. Instead of comparing images of the entire page, a component-based tool allows you to capture individual sections of a web page and compare them. This creates more focused tests and removes the false positives when something at the top of the page pushes everything else down, and everything comes back as changed.

CSS unit testing
Quixote (*https://github.com/jamesshore/quixote*) is an example of a unique class of diffing tools that look for unit differences instead of visual differences. Quixote can be used to set TDD-style tests where the test describes values that should be expected (title font-size is 1em, sidebar margin is 2.5%) and checks the web pages to see if those assertions are in fact true. This is a great approach for testing trouble areas such as the width of columns in a layout that keeps breaking. Or it can be used to assert that branding protocol has been followed and the logo is the correct size and distance away from other content.

Headless browser driven

Gemini (*https://github.com/bem/gemini*) is a comparison tool that can use PhantomJS (*http://phantomjs.org/*), a headless browser, to load web pages before taking screenshots. PhantomJS is a JavaScript implementation of a WebKit browser. This means that it is incredibly fast, and consistent across various platforms.

Desktop browser driven

Gemini is unique in that it also supports running tests using traditional desktop browsers. To do so, Gemini uses a Selenium (*http://docs.seleniumhq.org/download/*) server to open and manipulate the OS's installed browsers. This isn't as fast as a headless browser, and is dependent on the version of the browser that happens to be installed, but it is closer to real-world results and can catch bugs that might have been introduced in just a single browser.

Includes scripting libraries

CasperJS (*http://casperjs.org/*) is a navigation and scripting library that works with headless browsers like PhantomJS. It allows tools to interact with the pages opened in the browser. With CasperJS, you can move the mouse over a button, click on the button, wait for a modal dialog, fill out and submit a form, and finally, take a screenshot of the result. CasperJS even lets you execute JavaScript on the pages within PhantomJS. You can hide elements, turn off animation, or even replace always-changing content with consistent, mock content to avoid failures when the "newest blog post" gets updated.

GUI-based comparison and change approval

Projects like Diffux (*https://github.com/diffux/diffux*) store test history, and provide test feedback inside of a web-based graphical user interface. Baseline images are stored in a database, and any changes to those baselines must be approved or rejected inside of the app. These types of tools are great when you have nontechnical stakeholders needing to make the final decision on whether the changes are correct or not.

Command-line comparison and change approval

PhantomCSS (*https://github.com/Huddle/PhantomCSS*) is a component-based diffing tool, using PhantomJS and CasperJS, that runs solely in the command line. Test runs are initiated via a terminal command, and the results, passing or failing, are also reported in the terminal. These types of tools work especially well with task runners like Grunt or Gulp, and their output is well suited for automation environments like Jenkins or Travis CI.

We'll cover PhantomCSS and how to integrate it into your project in the next chapter, which takes a look at Red Hat's approach to testing.

CHAPTER 14

Red Hat Testing

Visual Regression in Action

PhantomCSS has been my go-to tool for the past few years because it provides component-based comparison, with a headless browser and scripting library that can be integrated with my current build tools. So let me walk you through the setup of PhantomCSS and how we are currently using it at Red Hat.

The Testing Tools

PhantomCSS (*https://github.com/Huddle/PhantomCSS*) is a powerful combination of three different tools:

- PhantomJS (*http://phantomjs.org/*) is a headless WebKit browser that allows you to quickly render web pages, and most importantly, take screenshots of them.
- CasperJS (*http://casperjs.org/*) is a navigation and scripting tool that allows you to interact with the page rendered by PhantomJS. We are able to move the mouse, perform clicks, enter text into fields, and even perform JavaScript functions directly in the DOM.
- ResembleJS (*http://huddle.github.io/Resemble.js/*) is a comparison engine that can compare two images and determine if there are any pixel differences between them.

We also wanted to automate the entire process, so we pulled PhantomCSS into Grunt (*http://gruntjs.com/*) and set up a few custom Grunt commands to test all, or just part, of our test suite.

Setting Up Grunt

Now before you run off and download the first Grunt PhantomCSS you find on Google, I'll have to warn you that it is awfully stale. Sadly, someone grabbed the prime namespace and then just totally disappeared. This has led to a few people taking it upon themselves to continue on with the codebase, merging in existing pull requests and keeping things current. One of the better ones is maintained by Anselm Hannemann (*https://github.com/anselmh/grunt-phantomcss*). Here's how you install it:

```
npm i --save-dev git://github.com/anselmh/grunt-phantomcss.git
```

With that installed, we need to do the typical Grunt things like loading the task in the *Gruntfile.js*:

```
grunt.loadNpmTasks('grunt-phantomcss');
```

Then set a few options for PhantomCSS, also in the *Gruntfile.js*. Most of these are just default:

```
phantomcss: {
  options: {
    mismatchTolerance: 0.05,
    screenshots: 'baselines',
    results: 'results',
    viewportSize: [1280, 800],
    },
    src: [
      'phantomcss.js'
    ]
},
```

- `mismatchTolerance:` We can set a threshold for finding visual differences. This helps account for antialiasing or other minor, noncritical differences.
- `screenshots:` Choose a folder to place baseline images in.
- `results:` After we run comparison tests, the results will be placed in this folder.
- `viewportSize:` We can always adjust the viewport size with Casper.js.
- `src:` This is just a path to our test file, relative to our gruntfile.

Our Test File

Next, in the *phantomcss.js* file, this is where Casper.js kicks in. PhantomCSS is going to spin up a PhantomJS web browser, but it is up to Casper.js to navigate to a web page and perform all of the various actions needed. We decided the best place to test our components would be inside of our style guide. It shared the same CSS with our live site, and it was a consistent target that we could count on not to change from day to day. So we start off by having Casper navigate us to that URL:

```
casper.start('http://localhost:9001/cta-link.html')
.then(function() {
  phantomcss.screenshot('.cta-link', 'cta-link');
})
.then(function() {
  this.mouse.move('.cta-button');
  phantomcss.screenshot('.cta-link', 'cta-link-hover');
});
```

After starting up Casper at the correct page, we use JavaScript method chaining to string together a list of all the screenshots we need to take. First, we target the `.cta-link` and take a screenshot. We aptly call it `cta-link`. That will be its base filename in the baselines folder.

Figure 14-1. The baseline image for our cta-link

Next, we need to test our button to make sure it behaves like we'd expect when we hover over it. We can use CasperJS to actually move the cursor inside of PhantomJS so that when we take our next screenshot, named `cta-link-hover`, the button will be in its hovered state. Figure 14-2 shows the result.

Figure 14-2. The baseline image for our cta-link in hovered state

Making a Comparison

With those baselines in place, we are now able to run the test over and over again. If nothing has changed, images created by the subsequent tests will be identical to the baseline images and everything will pass. But if something were to change:

```
.cta-link {
    text-transform: lowercase;
}
```

The next time we ran our comparison tests, we'd see the results shown in Figure 14-3.

Figure 14-3. An example of a failing test

As expected, the change from uppercase to lowercase created a failure. Not only was the text different, but the button ended up being smaller. The third "fail" image shows us in pink which pixels were different between the two images.

Running the Entire Suite

After doing this for each component (or feature) we want to test, we can run $grunt phantomcss and it will do the following:

1. Spin up a PhantomJS browser.
2. Use CasperJS to navigate to a page in our style guide.
3. Take a screenshot of a single component on that page.
4. Interact with the page: click the mobile nav, hover over links, fill out a form, submit the form, and so on.
5. Take screenshots of every one of those states.
6. Compare all of those screenshots with baseline images we captured and committed when the component was created Figure 14-4.

7. Report if all images are the same (PASS!) or if there is an image that has changed (FAIL!).
8. Repeat this process for every component and layout in our library.

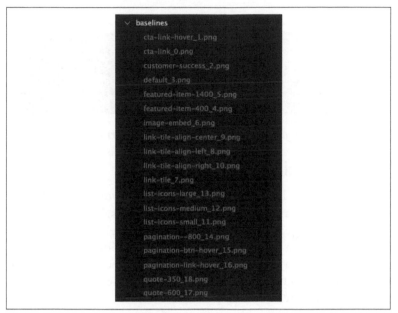

Figure 14-4. All of the baseline images created by our visual regression test

What Do We Do with Failing Tests?

Obviously, if you are tasked with changing the appearance of a component you are going to get failing tests, and that's fine (see Figure 14-5). The point is that you should only be getting failing tests on the component you are working on. If you are trying to update the cta-link and you get failing tests on the cta-link *and* your pagination component, one of two things happened:

- You changed something you shouldn't have. Maybe your changes were too global, or you fat-fingered some keystrokes in the wrong file. Either way, find out what changed on the pagination component, and fix it.
- On the other hand, you might determine that the changes you made to the cta-link should have affected the pagination too. Perhaps they share the same button mixin, and for brand con-

sistency they should be using the same button styles. At this point, you'd need to head back to the story owner/designer/person-who-makes-decisions-about-these-things and ask if the changes were meant to apply to both components, and act accordingly.

```
Failure! Saved to /Users/mgodbolt/Sites/webux/baselines/cta-link-hover_1.fail.png
Visual change found for cta-link-hover_1.png (47.62% mismatch)
Failure! Saved to /Users/mgodbolt/Sites/webux/baselines/cta-link_0.fail.png
Visual change found for cta-link_0.png (47.45% mismatch)
Failure! Saved to /Users/mgodbolt/Sites/webux/baselines/pagination--800_14.fail.png
Visual change found for pagination--800_14.png (26.92% mismatch)
Failure! Saved to /Users/mgodbolt/Sites/webux/baselines/pagination-btn-hover_15.fail.png
Visual change found for pagination-btn-hover_15.png (42.57% mismatch)
```

Figure 14-5. Seeing failures reported on subsequent runs

Moving from Failing to Passing

Regardless of what happens with the pagination, you will still be left with a "failing" cta-link test because the old baseline is no longer correct. In this case, you would delete the old baselines and commit the new ones (see Figure 14-6). If this new look is the brand-approved one, then these new baselines need to be committed with your feature branch code so that once your code is merged in, it doesn't cause failures when others run the test.

```
Changes to be committed:
  (use "git reset HEAD <file>..." to unstage)

        modified:   baselines/cta-link-hover_1.png
        modified:   baselines/cta-link_0.png
        modified:   baselines/pagination--800_14.png
        modified:   baselines/pagination-btn-hover_15.png
```

Figure 14-6. Commit new baseline images when your code changes the component appearance

The magic of this approach is that at any given time, every single component in your entire system has a "gold standard" image that the current state can be compared to. Your test suite can also be run at any time, in any branch, and it should always pass without a single failure, which is a solid foundation to build upon.

Making It Our Own

I started to work with Anselm's code at the beginning of the Red Hat project and found that it met 90% of our needs, but it was that last

10% that I really needed to make our workflow come together. So as any self-respecting developer does, I forked it and started in on some modifications to make it fit our specific implementations. Let me walk you through some of those changes that I made to create the node module @micahgodbolt/grunt-phantomcss (*https://www.npmjs.com/package/@micahgodbolt/grunt-phantomcss*):

```
// Gruntfile.js
phantomcss: {
  webrh: {
    options: {
      mismatchTolerance: 0.05,
      screenshots: 'baselines',
      results: 'results',
      viewportSize: [1280, 800],
    },
    src: [
      // select all files ending in -tests.js
      'src/library/**/*-tests.js'
    ]
  },
},
```

Place Baselines in Component Folder

Good encapsulation was important to us. We put everything in the component folder, and I mean everything! For example:

- The Twig template with the component's canonical markup
- The JSON schema describing valid data for the template
- The documentation file, which fed into our Hologram style guide explaining component features, options, and implementation details
- Sass files for typographic and layout styles
- The test file with tests written for every variation of the component

Because we already had all of this in one place, we wanted our baseline images to live inside of the component folder as well. This would make it easier to find the baselines for each component, and when a merge request contained new baselines, the images would be in the same folder as the code change that made them necessary.

The default behavior of PhantomCSS was to place all of the baselines into the same folder regardless of the test file location. With dozens of different components in our system, each with several tests, this process just didn't scale. So one of the key changes I made was to put baseline images into a folder called *baseline* right next to each test file (see Figure 14-7).

Figure 14-7. A typical component folder

Run Each Component Test Suite Individually

In addition to changing the location of the baseline images, I changed the test behavior to test each component individually, instead of all together. So, instead of running all 100+ tests and telling me if the build passed or failed, I now get a pass/fail for each component, as shown in Figures 14-8 and 14-9.

```
Running "phantomcss:webux" (phantomcss) task
No changes found for cta-link.png
No changes found for cta-link-hover.png
>> All 2 tests passed!
No changes found for pagination--800.png
No changes found for pagination-btn-hover.png
No changes found for pagination-link-hover.png
>> All 3 tests passed!
```

Figure 14-8. Everything passes!

```
Running "phantomcss:webux" (phantomcss) task
Failure! Saved to /Users/mgodbolt/Sites/webux/baselines/cta-link.fail.png
Visual change found for cta-link.png (47.45% mismatch)
Failure! Saved to /Users/mgodbolt/Sites/webux/baselines/cta-link-hover.fail.png
Visual change found for cta-link-hover.png (47.62% mismatch)
>> 2 tests failed.

Failure! Saved to /Users/mgodbolt/Sites/webux/baselines/pagination--800.fail.png
Visual change found for pagination--800.png (26.92% mismatch)
Failure! Saved to /Users/mgodbolt/Sites/webux/baselines/pagination-btn-hover.fail.png
Visual change found for pagination-btn-hover.png (42.57% mismatch)
No changes found for pagination-link-hover.png
>> 2 tests failed.
Warning: Task "phantomcss:webux" failed. Use --force to continue.
```

Figure 14-9. Failing tests

Test Portability

The last change I made is that I wanted my tests to be more portable.
Instead of a single test file, we had broken our tests up into dozens
of different test files that Grunt pulled in when it ran the test.

The original implementation required that the first test file start
with `casper.start('http://mysite.com/page1')` and all subsequent files start with `casper.thenOpen('http://mysite.com/
page2')`. This becomes problematic because the order in which
Grunt ran these files was alphabetical. So as soon as I added a test
starting with a letter one earlier in the alphabet than my current
starting test, my test suite broke!

The fix involved calling `casper.start` as soon as Grunt initiates the
task, and then all of the tests can start with `casper.thenOpen`:

```
// cta.tests.js
casper.thenOpen('http://localhost:9001/cta.html')
    .then(function () {
        this.viewport(600, 1000);
        phantomcss.screenshot('.rh-cta-link', 'cta-link');
    })
    .then(function () {
```

```
        this.mouse.move(".rh-cta-link");
        phantomcss.screenshot('.rh-cta-link', 'cta-link-hover');
    });

// quote.tests.js
casper.thenOpen('http://localhost:9001/quote')
    .then(function () {
        this.viewport(600, 1000);
        phantomcss.screenshot('.rh-quote', 'quote-600');
    })
    .then(function () {
        this.viewport(350, 1000);
        phantomcss.screenshot('.rh-quote', 'quote-350');
    });
```

Conclusion

After getting these tests in place, we were able to confidently grow our design system with new components, layouts, and patterns. With every addition of code, we had a suite of tests that ensured our previous work had not been compromised. Our coverage not only included the basic appearance, but every possible variation or interaction as well. As new features were added, new tests could be written. If a bug slipped through, we could fix it and then write a test to make sure it never happened again.

Instead of our design system getting more difficult to manage with every new addition, we found it getting easier and easier. We could now consistently utilize and adapt current components, or create new ones with little fear of breaking others.

PART V

The Documentation Pillar

Let's face it: our frontend code is getting more and more complex with every project we start. I'm not saying this is a bad thing, it's just that this rapid rate of growth comes with its own set of growing pains.

Just a few years ago all of our CSS was written in a single file, and each style used a long complex selector to find just the right element on the page to modify. If we found that this style was interfering with something else on our site, we just wrote another line of CSS at the bottom of the file with a longer selector.

In the same way, our JavaScript file was written using a bunch of jQuery functions targeting preexisting markup and applying some functionality to it. Each function would contain every bit of logic and processing required to get the job done. If we needed to write a slightly modified version of this functionality for another element, it was always easier to just duplicate the code, change the selector, and update the logic.

We were writing the equivalent of a single-file PHP application for every project.

Then, just as new PHP developers are taught to break up their code into small reusable objects and to organize their code into individual files, our frontend projects started to look less like a cascade of instructions and more like a complex system of abstraction, dependencies, and interfaces. But while we were quick to incorporate the object-oriented, multi-file approach of traditional programing languages, we were very slow to adapt their dedication to documentation.

We'd spent so many years living with highly declarative systems that we simply defaulted to keeping our understanding of these new systems locked away in our heads. Getting this information out of heads and into documentation won't be an easy transition, but the time lost from not having documentation outweighs the time it would have taken to write it. As the proverb goes, the palest ink is better than the best memory.

What Is Documentation?

Documentation is the blueprint of our design system. Without it, we will inevitably create solutions for problems that have already been solved and spend large amounts of time sifting through code to find the simplest answer. Without documentation, we leave our new hires scratching their heads as they wonder who could ever get work done in this system.

As we look back over all of the architecture we've established to this point, it would be criminal not to spend an equal amount of time planning our approach to documenting it. Documentation is part of development, not something to do after the important work is completed. Just like bloated code that needs refactoring, inefficient processes that could be automated, or functionality with no test coverage, skipping documentation creates technical debt.

Don't assume that documentation is simply writing down how things work. Yes, we need to establish time within our development process to document the things that we are building, but documentation is so much more than just writing a paragraph for each line of code we write.

Documentation comes in many forms, and many of those forms don't occur without some architectural intervention. While some documentation is just static text describing each function we write, it often has a build system behind it that layers on search, navigation, and visual presentation. Other documentation is used to display system assets, driven by the styles, scripts, templates, and schemas we are writing.

Static Documentation

Hologram (*https://github.com/trulia/hologram*) is a Ruby-based *general documentation* tool. It allows you to make small documentation entries all throughout your codebase, then it gathers them into a single static website. These Markdown-formatted documentation blocks can be placed right into your Sass, CSS, or JavaScript files. They are sprinkled with metadata that describes page name and navigation information, and they are a free-form space to write. Hologram allows your documentation to be inline with the code you are writing. This helps keep the documentation fresh and always in view of the developers.

SassDoc (*http://sassdoc.com/*) is a Node-based *system documentation* tool that claims to be "to Sass what JSDoc is to JavaScript," and it delivers! SassDoc is similar to Hologram in that it relies on inline blocks of comments to drive the finished documentation site. But where Hologram is very generic and multipurpose, SassDoc is focused on describing all of your Sass variables, functions, and mixins, and how they interconnect and depend upon each other. If you are building a large Sass framework, or creating a complex grid or color system, then SassDoc is the tool you'll want to pull out.

Code-Driven Documentation

Pattern Lab is a multiplatform *Pattern Library* tool that allows you to develop your design system in a modular approach and converts your templates and CSS into a browsable library of patterns. In modular design systems, you create each unique piece of the system once, and then combine them to create more complex patterns. Pattern Lab gives you a framework to build out those smaller pieces and combine them into complex patterns or even fully fleshed-out pages. This browsable component inventory is the perfect tool for developers, designers, UX, QA, and product owners to gather around. It creates a common language and common reference point for every piece of the design system.

JSON schema is a language for describing your data format, as well as a specification upon which you can validate your data. In the realm of frontend architecture, we can use JSON schema to document the data that each of our templates or patterns is expecting. A JSON hyper-schema can also be used to describe the various methods in which we can interface with our design system over HTTP, including validating, rendering, and testing. JSON schemas are code-driven documentation because they serve a functional purpose of validation and driving editor tools. Schemas also produce a very readable set of system specifications, replacing what is typically a large amount of handwritten instructions that developers would otherwise need to implement a feature.

CHAPTER 15

Style Guides

As our stylesheets evolve from a list of declarative statements to a system of variables, functions, and logic, we need to make sure that our documentation system evolves as well. Hologram (*http://trulia.github.io/hologram/*) equips us with everything we need to create a robust system of documentation for our design system. It allows us to annotate our system directly in the Sass or JavaScript files where we are writing our code. The annotation is automatically collected by Hologram and turned into a browsable website with rendered examples, as well as correlating code examples. This means that we aren't maintaining two separate codebases—the style guide is integrated into the actual design system. It is easy to see if code has been written without sufficient documentation.

On top of system documentation, Hologram allows us to create standard Markdown files that will be browsable within our style guide. These give us a great place to write onboarding docs, project rules and procedures, contact information, or anything else that needs to be captured, organized, and displayed for the team.

Let's take a quick look at the setup of Hologram and then jump into some documentation examples.

Hologram is a Ruby gem, so we'll start out by installing the gem to our system:

```
$ gem install hologram
```

Hologram Configuration

With the gem installed, we configure Hologram by creating a YAML file with the following:

```
destination: ./docs
documentation_assets: ./doc_assets
code_example_templates: ./code_example_templates
dependencies: ./build
source: ./sass
```

Let's take a closer look at each piece of code:

destination

This will be the folder in which Hologram builds our static style guide. If we are making this accessible to the outside world, this will be our public folder, and will hold everything we need to serve up our style guide.

documentation_assets

These are the static assets we'll be using to build our style guide. We'll need to specify the templates we are using to build the HTML, as well as any CSS or JavaScript we want to use to enhance the user's experience. This will include things like code highlighting, example layout, and navigation styles. If you aren't interested in building yet another site just to document your first one, you can always use one of the already built templates listed at the bottom of the Hologram GitHub page (*http://bit.ly/gh-hologram*).

code_example_templates

Code examples and how they render in the browser are the heart and soul of this style guide. Hologram provides a very easy way to customize the markup surrounding our examples. Here is the default markup that Hologram uses, which you could alter however you need:

```
<div class="codeExample">
  <div class="exampleOutput">
    <%= rendered_example %>
  </div>
  <div class="codeBlock">
    <div class="highlight">
      <pre><%= code_example %></pre>
    </div>
  </div>
</div>
```

Notice the two variables of `rendered_example` and `code_exam` `ple`. The rendered example is your example printed directly onto the page, whereas the code example is passed into a `<pre>` tag, properly escaped, and wrapped with code highlighting classes. Figure 15-1 shows an example set of rendered and example code.

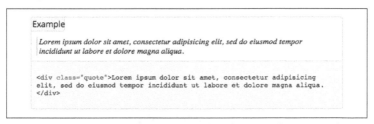

Figure 15-1. A quote component rendered in a Hologram style guide

`dependencies`

Similar to `documentation_assets`, `dependencies` describe a list of assets to be included in the style guide folder. These paths should include your compiled CSS, JavaScript, fonts, images, and any other asset needed to properly display and interact with your style guide content.

`source`

Lastly, we need to tell Hologram where to look for the documentation we want in our style guide. This array of sources can and should include your Sass/CSS, JavaScript/CoffeeScript, HTML templates, and icon font folders, as well as folders that might contain onboarding, workflow, or testing procedure information. Let's look at an example of documentation, what the values mean, and how it is rendered in the style guide.

Hologram Documentation Block

This example would be inside of your *_buttons.scss* file. The hologram content is put inside of a CSS comment, starting with the word "doc":

```
/*doc
---
title: Primary Button
category: Base CSS
---
```

```
    This is our button

    ```html_example
    <a class="btn" href="#">Click</a>
    ```
    */

    .btn {
      color: white;
      background: blue;
      padding: 10px;
      border: none;
      text-decoration: none;
    }
```

Let's take a look at each piece of this code.

Being Markdown, it enables us to include chunks of code, either inline or in blocks. Hologram comes with a custom Markdown renderer that uses a few block keywords (html_example, js_example, haml_example, and others) that will not only display the markup with syntax highlighting, but will also render the markup onto the page.

Figure 15-2 shows this button rendered in the Hologram style guide.

Figure 15-2. The primary button rendered in the style guide

title
: This is the human-readable title for this piece of documentation.

category
: Each category in your style guide will get its own page and entry in the navigation. You can put as many entries as you want into each category. The default template gives you jump links down to each documentation title.

Documentation body

> After the closing triple dash is the body of the documentation. This section is processed as Markdown, so we can easily include headings, lists, links, images or even tables without using a single HTML tag. But if we wanted to use HTML, that's completely fair game as well.

The Hologram Process

When Hologram runs, it looks through all the files in your source directory and pulls anything wrapped in /*doc */ into the style guide, using the YAML frontmatter to define its title and category. The end result is a build folder containing all of the dependencies (CSS, JavaScript, images) and an HTML file for each of your style guide categories.

Each page contains all of the documentation that matches that category, converted from Markdown and code blocks into standard HTML. The pages are then wrapped in the header and footer templates, pulling in CSS, JavaScript, fonts, and navigation elements. You can customize these templates to your heart's content, and if you are going to be spending much time in this style guide, you'll probably end up rewriting most of it, bringing in your own branding and styles.

Having our documentation block wrapped in comments is great because it means we can put our documentation right next to the code we are trying to document, but it will never affect the actual code used to style our design system. CSS comments are also easy to transport inside your module's CSS, and are very easy to strip out when you want to push out production code.

Hologram Conclusion

We are now able to write chunks of Markdown documentation right in our project source files. Hologram collects them all and converts them into a small website that we are able to customize, adding functionality like search or filtering, or styling to match corporate branding standards. Our documentation doesn't even have to be in the same file as the code it is documenting; we could break it out into a separate file next to our code. We have a separate docs file for each component that sits in the same folder as our styles. We also have documentation that has nothing to do with our Sass or

JavaScript, and is simply information on project setup and work-flow. We quickly found numerous uses for Hologram documentation, and I'm sure you'll find it just as useful as we did.

SassDoc

Hologram is a very free-form documentation system. It really doesn't care about its context, or what file the documentation is placed in. It also is a bit of a blank slate when it comes to theme. It's really only what you make it out to be.

SassDoc (*http://sassdoc.com/*), on the other hand, is the complete opposite. SassDoc, a tool for documenting your Sass's variables, mixins, extends, and functions, is very aware of the code that is directly after each comment block. It is also very opinionated in how the documentation is presented and styled. Hologram only organizes documentation into groups, but SassDoc automatically maps the relationship between your variables and functions, or your mixins and extends. If you are writing a large, Sass-based design system or a Sass framework, and you don't want to be writing all of your documentation by hand, then SassDoc is the tool for you! So let's look at how to get started with SassDoc.

Installing SassDoc

SassDoc is a NodeJS-based documentation system, and has plug-ins for Grunt, Gulp, and Broccoli. You can also run SassDoc from the command line with nothing other than a Sass file in your project. The output will always be the same, so for simplicity I'll demonstrate the command-line option. This way you can start playing with SassDoc right away without making changes to your project.

We start off by installing SassDoc as a global NPM package (again, this makes trying out SassDoc easier, but if you are going to use this in production you probably won't be using the global version):

```
$ npm install sassdoc --global
```

With SassDoc installed into your global NPM folder, you are now able to run the `sassdoc` command directly on your *sass* folder:

```
sassdoc sass
```

And that's it! SassDoc will search through all of the files in your *sass* folder and extract anything you have tagged with SassDoc's special

---

documentation syntax. It will then use all of that information to build out a fully featured static documentation site. Let's dive right into SassDoc's syntax, and see what our documented code looks like once processed.

Using SassDoc

SassDoc uses a three-slash Sass comment to let us signify that the following code needs to be included into our documentation. All you need to do is place `///` on the line above a mixin, extend, function, or variable, and SassDoc will do the rest. Here's an example using just a couple variables:

```
///
$button-padding: 1em;
$button-font-size: 1.2em;
```

In the preceding example, the `$button-padding` variable will be pulled into SassDoc, but the `$button-font-size` will not. SassDoc is smart enough to just grab the immediately following variable. Even if you put both variables on the same line in the file, SassDoc will still only import the first one. If you want to import both, just do the following:

```
///
$button-padding: 1em;

///
$button-margin: 1.2em;
```

With nothing more than two variables, six slashes, and a terminal command, SassDoc creates the documentation shown in Figure 15-3.

Wow! We didn't create a single template file or write a single line of CSS and we already have extremely professional-looking documentation built out of static HTML, CSS, and JavaScript. With a simple push to GitHub pages, you now have documentation that displays a list of your system's variables. But SassDoc does way more than that! We're just getting started.

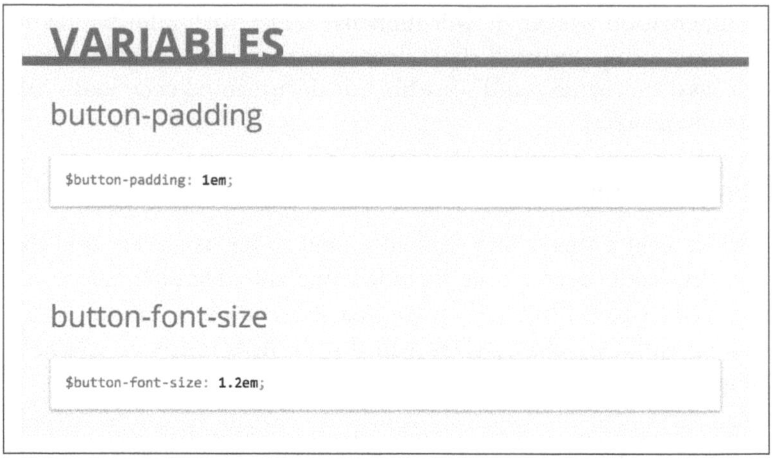

VARIABLES

button-padding

```
$button-padding: 1em;
```

button-font-size

```
$button-font-size: 1.2em;
```

Figure 15-3. A rendered SassDoc style guide

Exploring SassDoc

Let's create another variable and look at some of the annotation types SassDoc ships with:

```
/// A number between 0 and 360 used to find __foreground color__
/// @type Number
/// @access private
$foreground-adjust: 180 !global;
```

The variable shown here is preceded by SassDoc's triple-slash notation, but there are also a few lines of annotation that will be pulled in along with the variable name and value.

The first line of the doc block is always the description that SassDoc will display above the variable. This can be multiple lines, and is compiled as Markdown, so it supports headings, lists, links, and anything else you want to throw at it. Just make sure that each line is preceded by the three slashes.

After the description, we are free to use one of SassDoc's numerous annotation types. First up is the @type annotation. If this variable is simply a reference to another variable, or possibly the result of a function, it is helpful to describe whether this variable is a string, number, Boolean, or map. You can actually use any text string you like to describe the @type, so write what will be most useful for the reader.

The next annotation we've used here is `@access`. This annotation has two possible values: private and public. If you come from a traditional object-oriented programming background, you'll be familiar with the idea that you can set variables and functions as private, which means they are only accessible from within that object and cannot be called by other parts of the system. Sass doesn't actually have this type of technical restriction, but if you are creating variables, functions, mixins, or extends that only have internal uses, you should set the `@access` to private. This makes no functional change to your system, but it does tell users not to use this variable in their stylesheets, as it could be changed, removed, or refactored at any time.

As you can see in Figure 15-4, our `@access private` has set a [Private] flag on the variable title, our description is rendered with all of its Markdown glory, and our type is specified below.

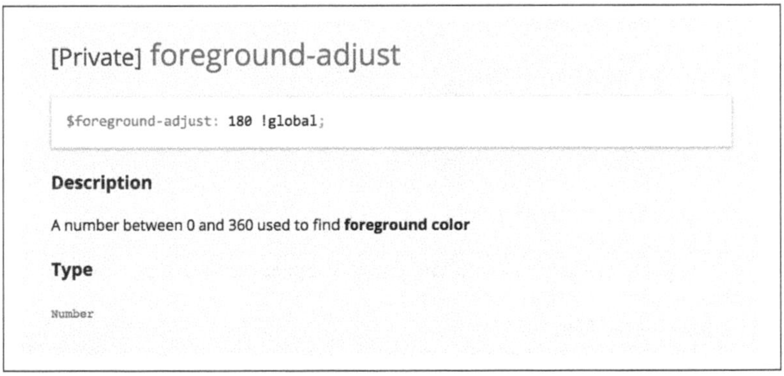

```
[Private] foreground-adjust

  $foreground-adjust: 180 !global;
```

Description

A number between 0 and 360 used to find **foreground color**

Type

Number

Figure 15-4. Our $foreground-adjust variable rendered in SassDoc

Digging Deep into SassDoc

Now that we've seen the basics for documenting our Sass design system, let's jump ahead and see how this looks when we have a more complete set of variables, functions, mixins, and extends. The following is a slightly contrived button mixin accompanied by everything it needs to output our button CSS:

```
/// Our global button padding
/// @access private
$button-padding: 1em !global;

/// Our global button font-size
/// @access private
```

```scss
$button-font-size: 1.2em !global;

/// A number between 0 and 360
/// @type number
/// @access private
$foreground-adjust: 180 !global;

/// Function to return a foreground color based
 on a background color
/// @access private
/// @param {color} $color - The background color
/// @return {color}
/// @example
///    @function get_foreground(blue);
///    // yellow
@function get_foreground($color) {
  @return adjust_hue($color, $foreground-adjust);
}

/// Our core button styles
/// @access private
%btn-core {
  padding: $button-padding;
  text-decoration: none;
  font-size: $button-font-size;
}

/// Our basic button mixin
/// @access public
/// @param {Color} $bg_color [red] - Background Color
@mixin button($bg_color:"red") {
  background: $bg_color;
  color: get_foreground($bg_color);
  @extend %btn-core;
}
```

Sitting among variables, functions, and extends, our `@mixin button` is the only publicly exposed part of this system. This ensures that our users will only call this mixin, and will never `@extend %btn-core`, call the `get_foreground` function, or use any of our variables. When we decide to refactor our button mixin, we know that we can remove or change any of these private elements without fear of breaking our code.

Our button mixin is using the `@param` annotation, which lets us document the various inputs that our mixin takes, and will display them in a nice, consistent format. The `@param` line is formatted like the following:

```
@param {type} $param_name [default value] - description
```

Internal Dependencies

One of the more powerful parts of SassDoc is its ability to automatically list internal dependencies. Without the %btn-core silent extend, our button mixin would break. Our button mixin is actually dependent on the get_foreground function as well, and SassDoc is able to track all of those dependencies and list them right at the bottom of the mixin documentation.

Putting everything together, Figure 15-5 shows what the button documentation looks like.

Figure 15-5. Our button mixin rendered in SassDoc

The %btn-core placeholder doesn't use any new annotation types, but as it is a dependency of our button mixin, and is dependent on a few of our variables, those relationships are spelled out automatically for us, as shown in Figure 15-6.

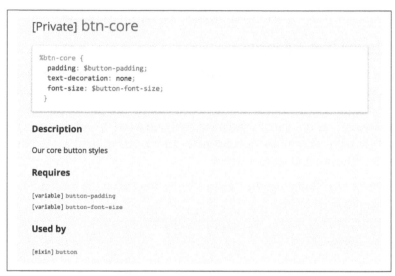

Figure 15-6. Our %btn-core extend, rendered in SassDoc

As shown in Figure 15-7, our `get_foreground()` function shows an example of the `@return` annotation, allowing us to describe what type of value we can expect to be returned from the function. It is also using the `@example` annotation that lets us write an indented block of code demonstrating how the function is used and what return we'd expect if we followed that example. Notice also the "Requires" and "Used by" sections. These automatically generated relationships are incredibly valuable, and as each one of them is a link to the mixin or variable definitions, it makes your documentation incredibly easy to navigate.

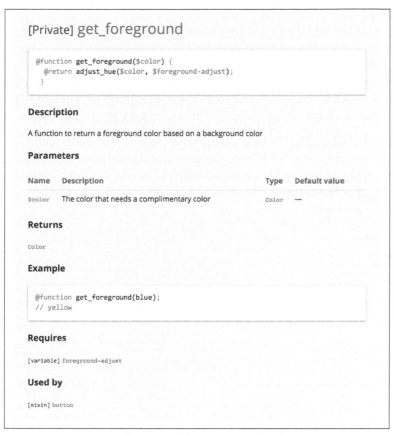

[Private] get_foreground

```
@function get_foreground($color) {
  @return adjust_hue($color, $foreground-adjust);
}
```

Description

A function to return a foreground color based on a background color

Parameters

Name	Description	Type	Default value
$color	The color that needs a complimentary color	Color	—

Returns

Color

Example

```
@function get_foreground(blue);
// yellow
```

Requires

[variable] foreground-adjust

Used by

[mixin] button

Figure 15-7. Our get_foreground function rendered in SassDoc

Conclusion

As the examples in this chapter demonstrate, static documentation systems can be a powerful way of capturing the ins and outs of your design system. Hologram provides the tools to create a very open and customizable set of documentation pages. Whether you are writing onboarding docs or capturing the proper markup for a call-to-action button, Hologram will give you the flexibility to write, catalog, and present it in style.

If you are looking for a documentation tool to create a more opinionated and standardized view of your Sass system, then SassDoc is the perfect tool to get you up and running. Even though it is still a static documentation tool, it brings a level of automation to your documentation by connecting system dependencies.

In no way are these two tools exclusive either. Many modern style guides are composed of several tools used to present each part of the system in the best possible manner. What these two systems do have in common, though, is that they rely on a significant amount of user input to achieve their true potential. As static documentation tools, they provide a way for us to write about the things we are building, and have all of that information gathered, cataloged, and indexed.

On the other side of the spectrum is a code-driven documentation system. In a code-driven environment, our documentation is driven purely by the code that we write. We'll talk about a couple examples of that in the following chapters.

CHAPTER 16

Pattern Libraries

In case you haven't come across Brad Frost's Atomic Design principles (*http://patternlab.io/about.html*), let me give you a quick introduction. They will without doubt change the way that you look at a website design, so you should take a much deeper dive into them when you get a chance.

Atomic Design is a methodology used to construct web design systems. Instead of designing entire pages one at a time, Atomic Design starts by breaking down commonly used elements into different sized patterns, and describes a process for combining these building blocks back together until we form an entire page. The smallest of these patterns, the element that cannot be broken down any further, is called the atom.

Atoms are the basic building blocks of our websites, composed of headings, list styles, images and videos, and form elements.

Just like atoms in nature combine to create things more complex, Atomic Design combines multiple atoms into *molecules*. A molecule might represent a search form, a media block, or a navigation system.

In the same way that molecules are created from combinations of multiple atoms, an *organism* comprises multiple molecules in order to create a "distinct section of an interface" like a blog article or comment.

Lastly, we create *templates*, which represent the combination and layout of multiple interface elements on a single page, including navigation, content, and footer elements.

What Is Pattern Lab?

Now that Atomic Design has equipped us with a methodology for creating our website out of small composable pieces, wouldn't it be great if we had a tool that allowed us to prototype new page designs with ease? This is where Pattern Lab steps in.

Pattern Lab (or PL) is a static site generator that allows you to document all of the building blocks of your site. It turns your atoms, molecules, organisms, and layouts into a browsable website where you can not only view each atomic component, but also create example pages that use custom content to mimic your actual website.

Getting Started with Pattern Lab

Pattern Lab is a small website of its own with CSS, Mustache templates, JSON data files, and a build system used to create the browsable static files. The original implementation was in PHP, but the demo I am about to show comes from the Node port of the project. Getting started typically involves cloning the repo directly into your project, or you can use something like Yeoman to quickly spin a new one up for you.

The best way to use Pattern Lab is to place it inside of your current project's theme directory, or at least put it somewhere where it can share files with the project. We do this to ensure that Pattern Lab and your website can share the same CSS and JavaScript files. This allows you to prototype inside of Pattern Lab, creating all of the necessary styles and scripts, and once the HTML is implemented in your CMS, all of the necessary CSS and JavaScript is already in place.

Once Pattern Lab is downloaded, and all of the associated Node modules installed (if you are using the Node version), you can spin up your PL website with a single command. For the Node version it is just $ grunt server. After a little compiling and spinning up a simple web server, we are treated with this: a prepopulated, simple style guide with sample atoms, molecules, organisms, templates, and even fully built pages, like the homepage in Figure 16-1.

Figure 16-1. The homepage preview in Pattern Lab

Pattern Lab in Action

The best way to understand what is going on under the hood is to start from this finished view, and work our way backward into the system of templates and data files that Pattern Lab holds. To do that, we are going to look at our hero image (the mountain) and see what it takes to get that image, with its headline, onto our page.

The first thing to understand is that these five different layers—atoms, molecules, organisms, templates, and pages—are all separated into their own folders, each pattern having a file that describes the markup that makes up that button, carousel, or footer navigation. At the pages level, where we take templates and add content to them, our patterns also have an associated data file, giving us an opportunity to replace the lorem ipsum with actual content. Let's take a look at this homepage pattern, and at the end of the rabbit hole, we'll find that there is an image tag for our snow-covered mountain view:

```
<!-- 00-homepage.mustache -->

{{> templates-homepage }}
```

As you can see, Pattern Lab uses Mustache files, which is a basic templating language, allowing us to use variables, iterate through sets of data, and import other files. In *00-homepage.mustache*, all we are doing is importing the homepage template, and nothing else. The reason we have "pages" is so that we can associate some data with the template, so let's take a look at part of that data file:

```
<!-- 00-homepage.json -->

{
  "title" : "Home Page",
  "bodyClass": "home",
  "hero" : [
    {
      "img": {
        "landscape-16x9": {
          "src": "../../images/sample/16x9-mountains.jpg",
          "alt": "Mountains"
        }
      },
      "headline" : {
        "medium" : "Top 10 mountain ranges for hiking"
      }
    }
  ],
  "touts" : [
    ...
  ],
  "latest-posts" : [
    ...
  ]
}
```

With this view of the data, we get a nice little skeleton outline of our page. We can see a title and a CSS class for the page, and we know that we are going to have a hero section followed by touts, and then our latest posts.

JSON (*http://www.json.org/*) is a great format for holding data. Strings are wrapped in quotation marks (""), arrays are wrapped in brackets ([]), and objects are wrapped in braces ({}). We can create an array of strings ["like", "this"] or even arrays of objects, which is what we just saw for each of our major sections, "hero," "touts," and so on.

So now that we have our data, let's dive into the first template that is called from our page, *templates-homepage*:

```
<!-- 00-homepage.mustache -->

<div class="page" id="page">
  {{> organisms-header }}
  <div role="main">
    {{# hero }}
      {{> molecules-block-hero }}
    {{/ hero}}
    <div class="g g-3up">
      {{# touts}}
        <div class="gi">
          {{> molecules-inset-block }}
        </div>
      {{/ touts}}
    </div><!--end 3up-->
    <hr />
    <div class="l-two-col">
      <div class="l-main">
        <section class="section latest-posts">
          <h2 class="section-title">Latest Posts</h2>
          <ul class="post-list">
            {{# latest-posts }}
              <li>{{> molecules-media-block }}</li>
            {{/ latest-posts }}
          </ul>
          <a href="#" class="text-btn">View more posts</a>
        </section>
      </div><!--end .l-main-->
      <div class="l-sidebar">
        {{> organisms-recent-tweets }}
      </div><!--end .l-sidebar-->
    </div><!--end .l-two-col-->
  </div><!--End role=main-->
  {{> organisms-footer }}
</div>
```

Homepage Template

The first thing you might notice about this template is that it is not actually named *template-homepage*. Pattern Lab uses a smart file resolution system, so instead of passing in an exact path, or even an exact filename, you write <type>-<name>. So when we need to import the header organism, we don't care that the filepath is actually *_patterns/02-organisms/00-global/00-header.mustache*, we only need to type {{> organisms-header }}.

After pulling in organisms-header, our template imports the page hero. Each section we import can be wrapped with a {{# }} tag to indicate a change in data context:

```
{{# hero }}
    {{> molecules-block-hero }}
{{/ hero}}
```

This means that when the block-hero molecule gets imported into the page, it will be using the data in the hero data object to render any variables:

```
{
  "img": {
    "landscape-16x9": {
      "src": "../../images/sample/landscape-16x9-mountains.jpg",
      "alt": "Mountains"
    }
  },
  "headline" : {
    "medium" : "Top 10 mountain ranges for hiking"
  }
}
```

Now that we know what data we'll be using, let's take a look at the *block-hero* Mustache file:

```
<div class="block block-hero">
 <a href="{{ url }}" class="inner">
    <div class="b-thumb">
      {{> atoms-landscape-16x9 }}
    </div>
    <div class="b-text">
      <h2 class="headline">{{ headline.medium }}</h2>
    </div>
 </a>
</div>
```

Our First Variables

This Mustache file holds our first variables. In Mustache, variables are words wrapped in {{ }}. The first variable, {{ url }}, you might notice, does not have an associated value in our set of data. If we wanted to specify the URL we would just need to add one more property to this data set with the key of url, and the template would pick up whatever value we tossed in:

```
{
    "url": "http://www.google.com",
    "img": {
        "landscape-16x9": {
            "src": "../../images/sample/16x9-mountains.jpg",
            "alt": "Mountains"
        }
    },
    "headline" : {
        "medium" : "Top 10 mountain ranges for hiking"
    }
}
```

However, because we didn't specify a value, Pattern Lab is smart enough to grab the default url value that we set in our global *data.json* file.

The next variable we see is {{ headline.medium }}, and this is a value that we do have. The dot notation means to look in the head line object for a property name of medium, and return that value, which is "Top 10 mountain ranges for hiking".

Going Atomic

The last template call needing to be resolved is the {{> atoms-landscape-16x9 }}. Just as we saw in the homepage template, this tag imports the "landscape-16x9" atom, but in this case we aren't changing the data context. This means that the Mustache file responsible for displaying the mountain image will use the exact same data that our block-hero is using. This shouldn't be a problem, as there is little chance of needing multiple img properties in our block-hero template. Therefore, using the same set of data as the block-hero, we call this template and pass in our mountain hero image:

```
<!-- 02-landscape-16x9.mustache -->
<img src="{{ img.16x9.src }}" alt="{{ img.16x9.alt }}" />
```

Pattern Lab lets us abstract out even the simplest piece of markup, and this image tag is a great example of that. Taking nothing more than our image source and an alt tag, this template might seem completely unnecessary. Why not just put the image tag into the block-hero like the H2 headline? In the end, it's always up to you and your team as to how much you want to abstract your templates, but the value of all image tags being produced by a single template can be quite significant.

Imagine that in the future you decide to add a class or data attribute to all of your image tags. If each template handled its own image tags, you'd be updating dozens of molecules. But if all images were handled by a single template, you could update it in one place and Pattern Lab would take care to distribute that atom anywhere it was used.

Running Off Atomic Power

Now that we've seen how the homepage hero graphic gets printed onto the page, we can take that same approach and break down every UI element on this page. The power of this approach is that as you continue to build, you quickly find that you can reuse pieces you've already built.

No longer are we approaching each page of a website as a blank slate, composed of unique markup and styles. We are getting to a point where we can create entire pages with the atoms, molecules, organisms, and templates that we already have in our system. And because everything on our website shares the same code, fixing the line height of a "published on" date doesn't require hunting down every page that implemented its own unique date field. We update the single atom, and those changes spread throughout the entire system.

The Pattern Lab documentation site is now a living, breathing, representation of every single building block your website uses. It catalogs brand colors, font families, logo specifications, and even animation examples. Because of this, Pattern Lab becomes one of the most complete and beneficial forms of documentation that your site can have. Not only is it a great development platform, but it acts as a common language for every member of your team.

Frontend development doesn't have to feel like we're constantly chasing our tails. If we are building pages, our work will only get harder over time. If we focus instead on building systems with tools like Pattern Lab, then our work actually gets easier over time. Now don't start worrying that we're working ourselves out of a job! Once we've freed ourselves from the tedium of building page-based websites, we can turn our focus to how we can make our systems even better. That's where JSON schemas come in. Instead of diving into a generic example here, I will take some time in Chapter 17 to explain how JSON schemas took Red Hat from a system like Pattern Lab to a fully integrated design system—a system that not only powers our style guide, but is also the basis of our content editing system, and the rendering engine for the majority of our site.

Red Hat Documentation

As I've looked back on the year-long process of developing the new design system for the Red Hat website, I realized that the entire project started with a need for documentation, and grew from there. The original request from management was to develop a style guide of our website's most commonly used bands, and make them available for other Red Hat web properties to use. It all started with a handful of Sass partials and a Hologram style guide, but it grew into so much more.

Stage 1: A Static Style Guide

As I wrote in Chapter 15, Hologram is a documentation tool that looks for specially marked comment blocks in your code, and converts the contents of those blocks into a style guide. Having heard about Hologram from Nicole Sullivan, I felt that it would be the perfect tool for us to document the layouts and components we were building.

Working inside of Hologram was quick and smooth. Each component or layout had its own Sass partial, so we placed our documentation block at the top of each file. The documentation included everything from our intentions for the component, to its capabilities and limitations, to a sample of the HTML markup. The markup allowed us to get a quick preview of the component without having to fire up the CMS, which made prototyping, cross-browser testing, and visual regression testing a lot easier.

Along with our library of components and layouts, we spent a great deal of time developing onboarding documentation, which explained not only how to set up this style guide, but how to use it, create new content for it, and push out new releases of it as well. Hologram was a great tool for this, as we could simply create a documentation folder, fill it up with Markdown files, and have Hologram pull them into our style guide based on how each page was categorized.

Everything was going just fine until we remembered that the original goal was to have a style guide that demonstrated how the code could be combined to create various commonly used patterns. This wasn't too difficult, as we just created a Patterns folder and started to create Markdown files with links to the components and layouts used in each pattern, including descriptions of which grid, alignment, and theme values were used. Once that was created, we went about copying and pasting the markup into the Markdown files, showing what a logo wall looked like, what HTML made up a featured video band, or the code differences in a featured event band when there were two events in the band versus three.

The problem was that each time we copy and paste markup from one place to another, the chance of that markup changing increases by a factor of a billion. It didn't take us very long to realize how unsustainable this approach was going to be, so we quickly looked for a solution where we could have a single canonical source of markup, and reuse that snippet anywhere we wanted to. Unfortunately, Hologram had no built-in support for any templating languages. I still have an open issue on the project's GitHub page from October 2014 asking about "processing html_example as ERB, to allow for reuse and template inheritance." (*https://github.com/trulia/hologram/issues/159*)

The solution we came up with was to use the Twig templating engine to process all of our documentation pages before passing them into Hologram. I was surprised to find that Twig had no issue processing a Markdown file, so here is a quick example of what the documentation would look like:

```
<!-- cta.docs.md -->

---
hologram: true
title: CTA Component
```

```
category: Component - CTA
---

- A "Call-to-Action" component contains one or more CTA buttons.

## Primary Button

```html_example
{% include "cta.twig" with {'type': 'primary'} %}
```

Secondary Button

```html_example
{% include "cta.twig" with {'type': 'secondary} %}
```

```html_example
<!-- cta.twig -->
<div class="rh-cta" >
 <a class="rh-cta-link" data-rh-cta-type="{{type}}" href="#">
  CTA Button
</a>
</div>

```
```

As you can see with this single page of documentation, we were able to use Twig's include function to print the same CTA markup in two different places, each with its own set of data. The resulting file was then passed on to Hologram to be processed normally:

```
<!-- cta.docs.md -->

---
hologram: true
title: CTA Component
category: Component - CTA
---

- A "Call-to-Action" component contains one or more CTA buttons.

## Primary Button

```html_example
<div class="rh-cta" >
 <a class="rh-cta-link" data-rh-cta-type="primary" href="#">
  CTA Button
</a>
</div>
```
```

```
## Secondary Button
```html_example
<div class="rh-cta" >
 <a class="rh-cta-link" data-rh-cta-type="secondary" href="#">
  CTA Button
 </a>
</div>

```
```

If we needed to make a change to the CTA markup, we could update a single Twig file, and our entire system would start using that new markup.

Stage 2: We Just Reinvented Pattern Lab

This was all well and good for single components, but eventually we started to document some of our layouts, like our card layout. A card is a simple layout that allows you to place multiple components into a padded box, and apply a theme and background. But if we were using Twig to import the card markup, how could we specify which components went into the card? We could just create a bunch of card templates, each one demonstrating a different combination of components, but there we are again copying markup!

The solution came in the fact that Twig allows us to pass in a variable to the include statement:

```
{% set template = 'cta.twig' %}

{% include template %}
```

This was exactly the power that we needed to create various examples of cards, each with different settings and content:

```
<!-- card.docs.md -->

---
hologram: true
title: Card Layout
category: Layout - Card
---

{%
 set data = {
   "theme": "dark",
   "components": [
     {
```

```
      "template": "image_embed.twig",
      "src": "my-image.jpg"
    },
    {
      "template": "cta.twig",
      "type": "primary"
    }
  ]
}
%}
```

```
{% include card.twig with data %}
```

```
<!-- end card.docs.md -->
```

```
<!-- card.twig -->
```

```
<div class="rh-card data-rh-theme="{{theme}}">
  {% for component in components %}
    {% include component.template with component only %}
  {% endfor %}
</div>
```

```
<!-- end card.twig -->
```

The preceding code does quite a bit of complex work, so let's break it
down, as this was the basis for our entire build system as we grew
from cards, to groups, to bands and beyond:

```
{% set

data = {
  "theme": "dark",
  "components": [
    ...
  ]
}

%}
```

Our first task is to create a data set that will describe what we want
to build. You can see we write some code that includes two properties: theme and components. While theme is just a string, our compo
nents property is an array holding two more objects, each with a
"template" property and other properties related to that template. If
you think this looks a whole lot like JSON, you are most certainly
correct. Though we started by using Twig data objects, we eventually converted to a JSON data workflow, but the logic remains the
same.

The next thing we need to do is include our card template using the data that we just set:

```
{% include card.twig with data %}
```

Lastly, let's take a look at the card's Twig file, and see how it handles this data we send over:

```
<div class="rh-card data-rh-theme="{{theme}}">

  {% for component in components %}
    {% include component.template with component only %}
  {% endfor %}

</div>
```

First thing we hit is the {{theme}} variable. That one's easy. We grab dark from the theme property, and that gets printed inside of our data attribute, just like we saw in the CTA Twig file.

The second bit of Twig we hit is slightly more complex. {% for com ponent in components %} means for each item in our components array (which we call component), do the following: import the template found in each array's template property, and pass the entire array into that template as the new data context. So first we import the *image_embed.twig* file and pass in an image source, then we import *cta.twig* and specify that we want the type to be primary:

```
{
  "template": "image_embed.twig",
  "src": "my-image.jpg"
},
{
  "template": "cta.twig",
  "type": "primary"
}
```

If this all sounds familiar to you, it's because you might have just read in the previous chapter how Pattern Lab is able to pass in a new data context to each atom or molecule that a layout imports. So if you are wondering...yes, we ended up creating our very own Pattern Lab.

I had many coworkers chuckle when they made the same realization, and they always asked why I didn't just use Pattern Lab in the first place. My original answer was simply that we came to this crossroads pretty organically. We started with one thing, and as our needs changed, we added functionality until we ended up with something that quite resembled Pattern Lab. But now I feel that what we built was much better suited for what we wanted to do.

Not only does Hologram provide us a place to store our Pattern Library, but we also were able to benefit from its ability to easily create a style guide and pages of pure documentation for things like installation, best practices, and deployment instructions. The other thing vastly different between our system and Pattern Lab is that in our system, all of our imports are determined by the data, and not hardcoded into the layout or organism like Pattern Lab.

This means that we were able to reuse our layouts for any combination of content we wanted to place inside of them, rather than having to rewrite the layout for each different combination of content we wanted to display. The other important thing to remember is that for us, once the rendering process begins, we have no control over the markup other than what is in this data. We don't have the option to tweak the source order of a layout for this one case, or add an extra container div to a component in another. These limitations, or restraints, are what ended up making our system as robust and powerful as it turned out to be. But before we got to that point, we needed to shed a bit of weight.

Stage 3: Splitting the Pattern Library from the Style Guide

One of my growing frustrations as our Pattern Library and style guide continued to grow was that in using a single Git repo we were constantly pushing up minor tweaks along with major overhauls to the style guide that had absolutely no effect on the Pattern Library itself. We were now well into a release schedule each sprint, and were pushing out prerelease Git tags every time we had a change. This caused quite a bit of confusion, as we had to determine if the new code actually affected the templates, styles, or JavaScript before bothering our backend developers with yet another prerelease. It also just felt dirty making tons of changes to a Git repo that would eventually end up in production just so that we could reorganize a few pages in the style guide.

The solution to this problem ended up providing way more benefits than we had initially expected. We decided to split our Pattern Library and style guide into separate repositories.

The instant benefit of this decision was that we could push changes to our style guide all day long without worrying about the effect of our changes on the production server. The Pattern Library now received far fewer pull requests, and we could better focus on how those changes might affect both production and our style guide, which were both importing the library via Bower.

The second benefit of this split was that now our production environment and our style guide were equal consumers of the Pattern Library. When we created a new band design in the style guide, the only tool we had for manipulating the markup was our JSON data array. We had no way of altering the markup or adding custom CSS for some special, one-off use case. This meant that anything we built in the style guide, we were confident could reproduce in production without modification to the templates.

At this point, our production environment was ingesting our CSS and JavaScript, but it had its own template-rendering engine that relied on PHP templates to do the heavy lifting. We had been able to faithfully replicate each layout and component in PHP, but it was a very manual process, and any change we wanted to make to our Pattern Library templates would have to be replicated in production.

This isn't an uncommon problem. Most Pattern Lab users, who are able to create various designs, patterns, and pages using the built-in Mustache templates, still pass over the compiled markup for the backend developer to implement. This doesn't mean that they like it! I'm sure they wish they could update an atom or molecule in their library and have their CMS pick up those changes and instantly start rendering pages with those changes.

Fortunately for us, we were already using Twig, which was built to compile in PHP, and we had some developers that were willing to create the missing link between our Pattern Library and the CMS rendering engine.

Stage 4: Creating a Unified Rendering Engine

One of the greatest struggles facing Drupal frontend developers is that we cannot replicate the incredibly complex rendering process Drupal uses to create markup without using Drupal itself. We are forced to either create static markup and pass it off for implementation, or we have to work with the markup rendered by the CMS, and create content in the CMS before we can even start writing styles.

But once we split the Pattern Library away from the style guide, we realized that we had created a brand-new Twig-powered rendering engine that could be used by both Drupal and our style guide. Given a set of JSON data passed into a Twig render function, our markup-as-a-service, or design API, would return the same markup every time. Our Pattern Library could now be installed into any system that could compile Twig. If the JSON data was collected and formatted correctly, the rendered HTML would be identical regardless of whether it was passed in from a static file, or created inside of a complex CMS.

The challenge, of course, was knowing what correctly formatted data looked like. What properties did each template accept? Were they strings, numbers, or Booleans, and which ones were required? Did any of them have restrictions on what values they accepted? How could we be sure that the data we were sending to Twig was actually valid, not to mention whether it would produce the desired HTML? Attempting to answer all of these questions led us to one of our greatest discoveries: JSON schemas.

JSON Schemas

Simply put, JSON schemas describe a set of data. To be more specific, in our Pattern Library, JSON schemas describe the data that a template file needs to render properly. It lists each template variable, which ones are required, the variable data type, and any restrictions that the value has.

If our card has a theme variable, our schema informs us that the theme variable is required and must be a string value of dark or light. If we try to omit the theme, or to pass a value of gray to the template, the card schema will return a validation error.

We can also use JSON schemas to indicate that our card can contain a number of different components, and we can validate a complex JSON array that we might use to render a complex band, all in a single pass. The following code might contain a valid card, but the CTA component inside of it is not valid because tertiary isn't an allowed type value:

```json
{
  "template": "band.twig",
  "theme": "dark",
  "components": [
    {
      "template": "cta.twig",
      "type": "tertiary"
    }
  ]
}
```

Because the JSON schema allows us to use references to describe the CTA you can put into a card, group, or band, we never have to duplicate our schema files, and just like Twig templates, we keep a single canonical source. Therefore, creating JSON schemas for everything from the smallest button to the largest layout, we now have an incredibly complex and comprehensive schema that can validate each and every band we want to render.

Armed with these schemas, our developers could now see at a glance the data needs for any template file, and could validate the data they were gathering before sending it over to our shared Twig rendering engine. This was a huge improvement from our older system in that they were no longer required to fiddle with the output markup until it matched what we had in the style guide. They could be confident that if their data validated, the rendering engine would return to the correct HTML. Unfortunately, there was still a problem with this approach.

Our developers were still saddled with creating the dozens of input fields required to capture the titles, images, and text paragraphs needed for each page. Once all of those fields were created, they would then laboriously map each one to the JSON array before rendering. They also had no way to reuse the fields used to capture data for each template file. Every time they gathered the text, href, and type of our CTA button, they had to create a brand-new set of fields in the CMS, which also required separate database entries.

Fortunately for us, JSON schemas had a few more tricks up their sleeves.

Stage 5: Automating the Creation of New Patterns

I am by no means an experienced backend PHP developer, but I hate repetitive tasks as much as the next person. I could really feel the pain of our developers who were configuring dozens and dozens of input fields just so that they would match the schemas I had already written. I also couldn't help but wonder how powerful our design system could be if the work that we did in schemas, templates, and styles could be automatically and programmatically imported into our CMS without a single hour of backend dev intervention.

What if there was no more waiting until the next three-week sprint to find a dev resource to implement our new pattern? What if we could eliminate "lost in translation" issues where the developer had to make an assumption about how the pattern worked, and the feature had to be pushed back a sprint to deal with a number of defects?

Jeremy Dorn's JSON-editor (*http://jeremydorn.com/json-editor/*) is a tool that takes a JSON schema and creates form out of the schema properties. It then returns the JSON data from the form as you update the form fields. We were using this tool in our Pattern Library to interact with the schema, templates, and styles, and get instant visual feedback of how changing a property affected the rendered results. We'd had great success with this editor and its ability to transform a schema into a set of editable fields, so we were pretty confident that the same approach could be applied to Drupal, or WordPress, or any other platform that wanted to use our design pattern.

Our faith in the power of the JSON schema was rewarded when our developers jumped on the opportunity to create an automated JSON schema importing process inside of Drupal. Within a few weeks, we had a system that automatically converted our components and layouts into Drupal entities. Now they were able to create a single entity for our CTA component, and reference that entity and its database fields each time that our little call-to-action button was required.

Creating Patterns

We also wanted to take advantage of the various Red Hat–branded patterns we created, which were specific recipes for putting layouts and components together. A pattern made assumptions about the grid layout, or the components used, or the values of some of the properties. This way if we needed to create a logo wall, which always contained image embeds, with five per row, we could simply use a pattern instead of setting all of those manually.

It turns out that patterns could also be written as JSON schemas. Each pattern band looked very similar to our canonical band schema, and described data that would always validate if passed through that schema. But it was more restrained than the band schema, and didn't always offer all the options for background, layout, or component selection.

So through the power of a simple set of JSON schemas, we were now in a position where we could not only prototype the design of a new component, but we could also define the actual template file that would be used to render that design, as well as the data model that would need to feed that template, and the UI that would allow us to collect all of that data!

Our decision to embrace JSON schemas, with all of the power they brought and restraints that they required, transformed our design system into what it is today. It started as nothing more than a collection of design elements and the markup that we hoped would be used in implementation, and it resulted in a streamlined and efficient prototyping-to-rendering pipeline that removed a great deal of repetitive work. It also allowed the work we did on the frontend to completely define the entire process of collecting, storing, rendering, and styling content inside of our CMS.

CHAPTER 18

Conclusion

One of the greatest lessons I have learned about frontend architecture over the life of this project is that, as with any good architect, your job is never finished until the last stone has been laid. We started this project with a very simple scope, and we created an architecture that met our needs at that time. But over time, our needs changed, the project evolved, and successes in one area turned into opportunities in others.

Sometimes I look back at all of the time we spent to get to this point and wonder why we didn't just do this in the first place. Why have we gone through so many iterations, rather than just architecting this finished product from day one? Does this mean we've failed, or that our work was for nothing? I am confident that this is not the case.

As we continue to learn about frontend architecture, I am certain that the time between project start and where we've gotten today will continue to get shorter, and that we'll get there in fewer iterations, though iteration will always be part of the process! As frontend architects, our job is to understand our current strengths and weaknesses, and to foresee possible opportunities and threats. The way that we foresee is to have already experienced. The way that we understand is to have already underestimated. The greatest talent that we can bring to the table is an understanding of how this crazy thing called frontend development comes together over time.

So if this is your first time creating an architectural plan, just know that you are going to need to iterate a lot! Don't place all of your hopes in a single solution, framework, or platform until it has proven itself to you time and time again. And if you have been doing this for a long time, you already know that we still have to be willing to iterate and try out new things. We don't walk into a new site build with an arsenal of table-based layout and static Photoshop comps, so never assume that the tool you've been using for the past several builds is still the best choice to get the job done.

But most of all, if you are feeling drawn to taking up the mantle of the frontend architect, remember that you are never alone. There are many practitioners of the art, regardless of the title that they hold.

Don't be afraid to ask for help. Don't be afraid to share what you learn. Don't be afraid to stand up on a stage and encourage others to follow this discipline. And no matter what you do, never under any circumstance be afraid to write it all down in a book.

Index

About the Author

Micah Godbolt, frontend architect, author, podcaster, trainer and speaker at worldwide open source events, is often found promoting frontend architecture, Sass, visual regression testing, and schema-based design at his blog, *https://micah.codes*. A Pacific Northwest native, he currently lives outside of Portland with his wife and two children.

Micah has worked as a contractor for Red Hat, Inc. However, the views expressed in this book are solely those of the author and do not reflect the views of any current or past employer, including Red Hat, Inc.

Colophon

The animal on the cover of *Frontend Architecture for Design Systems* is a pink-headed warbler (*Cardellina vericolor*). Found mostly in Guatemala and southern Mexico, pink-headed warblers are small passerine birds that prefer higher altitudes (5,900–11,500 feet).

Pink-headed warblers average about five inches in length and usually weigh about 10 grams. They are songbirds with a high metallic song that sounds like *tsiu* or *tseeip*. Only males sing, but both sexes use a lower chirping noise to stay in touch with their mates.

Unless they're feeding young chicks, it is rare to see two pink-headed warblers together. They generally prefer to perch in the dense understory of untouched cloud forests, but this kind of habitat is becoming more and more difficult to find throughout the bird's range. It is expected that as forests become more fragmented in Guatemala, this species will start to show up in El Salvador along with many others.

Male pink-headed warblers begin singing on the first good-weather days in February and continue for the next several months. Around the same time as the males begin to sing, the females begin to construct ground nests out of pine needles and moss. After mating, the female lays 2–4 eggs and incubates them for 16 days. After that, chicks are fed by their parents for 10–12 days before leaving the nest and learning how to hunt for insects on their own.

Get even more for your money.

Join the O'Reilly Community, and register the O'Reilly books you own. It's free, and you'll get:

- $4.99 ebook upgrade offer
- 40% upgrade offer on O'Reilly print books
- Membership discounts on books and events
- Free lifetime updates to ebooks and videos
- Multiple ebook formats, DRM FREE
- Participation in the O'Reilly community
- Newsletters
- Account management
- 100% Satisfaction Guarantee

Signing up is easy:

1. Go to: oreilly.com/go/register
2. Create an O'Reilly login.
3. Provide your address.
4. Register your books.

Note: English-language books only

To order books online:
oreilly.com/store

For questions about products or an order:
orders@oreilly.com

To sign up to get topic-specific email announcements and/or news about upcoming books, conferences, special offers, and new technologies:
elists@oreilly.com

For technical questions about book content:
booktech@oreilly.com

To submit new book proposals to our editors:
proposals@oreilly.com

O'Reilly books are available in multiple DRM-free ebook formats. For more information:
oreilly.com/ebooks

O'REILLY®

Have it your way.